Shining Moments

Visions Of The Holy
In Ordinary Lives

Cycle A

John E. Sumwalt, Editor

with

Ralph Milton, Rosmarie Trapp, Sandra Herrmann,
Pamela J. Tinnin, Richard H. Gentzler, Jr.,
David Michael Smith, Jody E. Felton, Nancy Nichols,
William Lee Rand, and others.

CSS Publishing Company, Inc., Lima, Ohio

SHINING MOMENTS

Copyright © 2004 by
CSS Publishing Company, Inc.
Lima, Ohio

Some scripture quotations are from the *New Revised Standard Version of the Bible*, copyright 1989 by the Division of Christian Education of the National Council of the Churches
of Christ in the USA. Used by permission.

Some scripture quotations are from the *King James Version of the Bible*, in the public domain.

Library of Congress Cataloging-in-Publication Data

Shining moments : visions of the Holy in ordinary lives, Cycle A / John E. Sumwalt, editor;
with Ralph Milton ... [et al.].
    p. cm.
  ISBN 0-7880-2327-6 (perfect bound : alk. paper)
1. Miracles. 2. Visions. 3. Common lectionary (1992). Year A. I. Sumwalt, John E. II. Milton,
Ralph. III. Title.

BT97.3.S55 2004
248.2—dc22

                                              2004014781

For more information about CSS Publishing Company resources, visit our website at
www.csspub.com or e-mail us at custserv@csspub.com or call (800) 241-4056.

ISBN 0-7880-2327-6
PRINTED IN THE U.S.A.

3-18-05

Dear Barb,

To a sister-in-Christ who I encourage to write YOUR story so that others will know that Jesus is living and working in you.

Love,
Laurie

To my mentor and friend, Kendall W. Anderson

As he came down with the two tablets of the covenant in his hand, Moses did not know that the skin of his face shone because he had been talking with God. When Aaron and all the Israelites saw Moses, the skin of his face was shining, and they were afraid to come near him.

— Exodus 34:29b, 30

And while he was praying, the appearance of his face changed, and his clothes became dazzling white ... Now Peter and his two companions were weighed down with sleep, but since they stayed awake, they saw his glory.... — Luke 9:29, 32a

Now as he was going along and approaching Damascus, suddenly a light from heaven flashed around him. He fell to the ground and heard a voice saying to him, "Saul, Saul, why do you persecute me?" He asked, "Who are you, Lord?" The reply came, "I am Jesus, whom you are persecuting."

— Acts 9:3-5

At once I was in the spirit, and there in heaven stood a throne, with one seated on the throne! And the one seated there looks like jasper and carnelian, and around the throne is a rainbow that looks like an emerald. — Revelation 4:2, 3

Religion starts, as Frost said poems do, with a lump
in the throat, to put it mildly, or with the bush going up in flames, the rain of flowers, the dove coming down out of the sky.

Frederick Buechner

Visions, even dramatic visions, are meant to be a
normal part of our spiritual experience. What's
needed is help in awakening our natural style of
sensing the holy so that each of us can take own-
ership of our own style of sacred seeing.

Eddie Ensley

> My hands stretch out and upward,
> Stretch as far as they will go.
> The light comes crashing through me
> Like an arrow from a bow ...
> The warmth of love surrounds me,
> For a part of me has died ...
> My heart is full of loving.
> My life has begun to grow.
>
> Gail Ingle

Frederick Buechner, *A Room Called Remember; Uncollected
Pieces* (New York; Harper and Row, 19920, p. 151.

Eddie Ensley, *Visions: The Soul's Path To The Sacred* (Chi-
cago: Loyola press, 2000), p. 32.

Gail Ingle is the author of "Dreams" in *Sharing Visions: Divine Revelations, Angels, And Holy Coincidences,* CSS Publishing Company, Inc., 2003, pp. 201-202, and "Metacosmic
Light" in this volume, on pages 27-28. Gail passed on June
13, 2004, at the age of 54 with a "heart full of loving."

Table Of Contents

Acknowledgments 11

Advent
Not Left Behind 15
  Nancy Nichols
Coventry Story 17
  Jody E. Felton
Right Here In My Church 20
  April McClure Stewart
Gram 23
  William Bell

Christmas
Christmas Presence 29
  Janice Hammerquist
Warnings 30
  Vickie Eckoldt
  Elaine Klemm Grau
A Dog Came For Christmas 32
  John Sumwalt

Epiphany
Metacosmic Light 37
  Gail C. Ingle
Your Dad Likes You 40
  Kathleen A. "Kit" Slawski
An Unexpected Song 41
  Derrick Sanderson
A Dog's Life 46
  David Michael Smith
A Comforting Dream 49
  Harold Klug
The Horse Whisperer 50
  William Lee Rand

An Old Enemy   53
Kendall W. Anderson
Discerning God's Direction   55
Jane Moschenrose
I Will Not Forget You   58
J. Michael Mansfield
Charlie Is Glowing   60
Deb Alexander

Lent

Still Learning Not To Wobble   65
Rosmarie Trapp
Born Again   68
Kathy Raines
Water Sign   69
Anne Sunday
The Gift Of Myself   72
Jim Eaton
The Wandering Eye   74
Paul Calkin

Holy Week And Easter

Forsaken?   79
Judith B. Brain
Easter Stories   80
Ralph Milton
Lisa Lancaster
Ned Dorau
Hoo   83
Claire Clyburn
Stranger In The Choir   86
Martha Hartman
Holy Hands   88
David Michael Smith
A Rock Of Refuge   92
Jody E. Felton
I Will Not Leave You Orphaned   96
Lori Hetzel

Lambasting God   99
  Maria Seifert
Kristina's Angel   103
  Theresa Hammerquist

Pentecost

Wrapped In Pentecost   109
  Kate Jones
God Created Death?   114
  John Sumwalt
Sufficient Grace   116
  Joyce Schroer
High And Lifted Up   118
  Laurie Woodard
I Gave You To God   120
  Andrew Oren
A Doula's Prayer   122
  LaNette J. McQuitty
A Cup Of Coffee   125
  Tom Kadel
Is God Listening?   129
  Barbara Frank
A Light To My Path   130
  Linda Willis Harper
A Father's Love, A Mother's Good-bye   132
  R. Ellen Rasmussen
Praying: Even When You Can't   135
  Pamela J. Tinnin
Too Churchy   138
  Paul Karrer
Angels In Haunted Places   140
  Richard H. Gentzler, Jr.
A Time To Weep   142
  Christina Berry
Help In The Name Of The Lord   144
  Sandra Herrmann
Response   147
  Marie Regine Redig

The Winds Of God   148
   Larry Winebrenner
Louise   154
   Kay Boone Stewart
Worth Waiting For   156
   Ruth F. Piotter
Nothing In My Brain   157
   Cindy Loomis-Abell
Looking Forward With Love   159
   Lois Ann Weihe Bross
Inside A Tornado   161
   Carolyn Peake
Is It Asking Too Much?   163
   C. B. "Cleve" Bishop
Prayer At Midnight   165
   Marjorie K. Evans
Stand Still And See!   167
   Bonnie Compton Hanson
That You May Not Grieve   169
   John Sumwalt
A Different Realm   171
   Susan D. Jamison
A Choice To Make   174
   Susan Monnarjahn
Together Again   177
   Barbara Frank
   Bonny Joy Bailey
An Overpowering Light   179
   Karen Steineke

U. S. / Canadian Lectionary Comparison 183

Contributors   185

Acknowledgments

It has been a joy to work with the sixty contributors to this third volume of vision stories. It is an honor and a privilege to have a part in the sharing of these witnesses. My thanks to each one of them for entrusting me with their sacred stories.

I am thankful for the encouragement and support of our publisher, Wesley Runk; our editors, Teresa Rhoads, Rebecca Brandt, and Stan Purdum; and to Ellen Shockey, Tim Runk, Jonathon Smith, David Jordan-Squire, Missy Cotrell, Bethany Sneed, Beth Diamond, and the rest of the hard-working CSS team.

This book would not have been possible without the wisdom and hard work of my writing partner of 29 years, Jo Perry-Sumwalt. She is a kind and loving editor, more than I deserve.

Special thanks to our colleagues on the Wauwatosa Avenue Church staff, Carol Smith, Mary Peterson, Janice Beutin, Jodie Hunt, and Don Truman.

Advent

Late have I loved you, O beauty so ancient and so
new. Late have I loved you! You were within me
while I have gone outside to seek you. Unlovely
myself, I rushed toward all those lovely things you
had made. And always you were with me, and I
was not with you.

Saint Augustine

Saint Augustine, *Confessions Of Saint Augustine*, Book X,
Ch. XXVI, in public domain.

Not Left Behind

Nancy Nichols

But about that day and hour no one knows, nei-
ther the Angels of heaven, nor the Son, but only
the Father. (v. 36)

I grew up in a family and church well centered in the Age of
Reason; thoughts and ideas gave validity to human experience.
My faith was well reasoned. It was historically based. It was ha-
bitual. I longed for more.

When I was in high school, a faith group based on charismatic
and apocalyptic faith experiences came to the area. The "cool"
kids joined in and so did many of my friends, which made them
cool as well. While I could not agree with them rationally, I found
myself drawn to the emotional expression of their faith and the
acceptance by peers who would once have ignored me. I still attended my United Methodist church, but I was certainly willing to
explore something more.

On New Year's Eve, 1975, this group of friends gathered together. We went to an Assembly of God worship service that focused on the coming of the end. They believed that 1976 would
bring the parousia, the rapture, the end, the second coming. I left
the church thinking, I'm only seventeen. There is way too much of
life left for me to experience. I don't want this yet! After leaving
the church, we spent the night at Jill's house. We stayed up talking
about all we had heard. My friends were convinced that this was
indeed the year. I wasn't so sure.

I went home the next morning, New Year's Day, 1976. I decided that I needed to read Revelation. So I started reading the
most complex book in the biblical record, on no sleep, with a heart
filled with fear! I made it about half way through before I fell into
a troubled sleep.

The house I grew up in was old and creaky. The steam heat made loud noises, the floorboards creaked, and the tree limbs just outside the windows rubbed together, making strange noises. Usually those sounds were the sounds of comfort. But on January 1, 1976, every noise that invaded my sleep brought fear. I was sure that each creak was the trumpet prelude to a mass rapture that would leave me behind to face enemy forces!

Then it happened. I had a dream. I had THE dream. In my dream, Jesus descended halfway, looked straight at me, and said, "Nancy, I love you, go back to sleep, don't worry, I'm not coming for a very long time, and I won't leave you behind." I fell into a deep sleep, and woke, refreshed.

Looking back, I realized that the dream was not just about the end of times, but about all of those times when I felt that Jesus was leaving me behind. That dream prepared me to face losing my mother just fifteen months later. That dream prepared me to move from being an adolescent to an adult. That dream allowed me to answer, finally, the call to ministry I first heard when I was twelve. That dream stayed with me during the dark nights of the soul when I could not find God. That dream is part of my faith. "Nancy, I love you, go back to sleep."

Coventry Story

Jody E. Felton

*The wolf shall live with the lamb, the leopard shall
lie down with the kid, the calf and the lion and the
fatling together, and a little child shall lead them
... They will not hurt or destroy on all my holy
mountain; for the earth will be full of the knowledge of the Lord as the waters cover the sea.*
(vv. 6, 9)

Terror fell from the sky. For hours during the night of November 14, 1940, the bombs fell on Coventry in central England. As
November 15 dawned, the whole city was ablaze. Coventry Cathedral died in the flames that night.

For the first time in history a whole city was destroyed from
the air. There would be others, but Coventry was the first. The
work of that night produced a new word — "coventrated."
"Coventrated" — meaning to "utterly destroy."

The aftermath of that night was silence ... shocked, horrified
silence. The survivors stood in the ashes of the rubble, numb and
bewildered. What had once been a prosperous industrial city lay
in ruins, the buildings flattened, the streets buried in rubble, the
whole city center razed to the ground.

What kind of hatred could produce such horror? More impor-
tantly, how was such hatred to be answered. Jesus said, "You have
heard it said, 'an eye for an eye, and a tooth for a tooth.' But I say
to you, do not resist evil. If one strikes you on the right cheek, turn
to him the other also." Would the people of Coventry be able to
hear those words? The city was utterly destroyed. Did they even
have another cheek to turn? On the morning of November 15 the
future of the people of Coventry hung in the balance. Would they

17

meet hatred with hatred, or hatred with hope? Would the city remain razed to the ground or raised to reconciliation?

The answer came when the Cathedral caretaker, Jock Forbes, found two charred beams from the Cathedral's fourteenth-century roof. Tying the two beams together, he formed a cross and set it up in the rubble. In planting that cross, Jock Forbes identified the mound of rubble with Calvary, the death of Coventry with the death of Jesus on the cross.

The Rev. A. P. Wale, a local priest, restated that understanding when he made a cross out of three nails from the Cathedral roof. The Cross of Nails has become the symbol of reconciliation for Coventry.

From those two crosses has grown the ministry of Coventry Cathedral, a ministry of hope and reconciliation. From those two crosses, made from the destruction of human hatred, a renewed understanding of the crucifixion and resurrection of Jesus has emerged. The people of Coventry discovered that forgiveness lies between crucifixion and resurrection, between hatred and hope, between death and new life, between being razed to the ground and raised to reconciliation. Out of the rubble an altar was made, inscribed with the words, "Father Forgive."

Today a new Cathedral rises up next to the ruins, a Cathedral filled with light and color and life. The light streams through the many stained glass windows, making deep pools of color on the floor. The art work and beautiful chapels speak of God's call to humanity, a call to love and wholeness.

The Cathedral congregation is active, with many diverse ministries, giving the Cathedral not only light and color, but life as well. They have refused to allow evil to turn their lives into bitterness and hatred. They have learned to forgive, but they do not forget. The whole back wall of the Cathedral is made of glass, etched with haunting figures of patriarchs, saints, and angels. That glass wall looks out onto the ruins of the old Cathedral. The people of Coventry have learned the fine balance of remembering and forgiving, allowing God to transform memories into a movement of reconciliation. They remember not so they can hold a grudge, but so that they may be instruments of God's action in the world.

Their understanding of their mission is summed up in the words found under the glass wall in the new Cathedral, "To the Glory of God this Cathedral that burnt November 14, 1940, A.D., was rebuilt in 1962." The new Cathedral rises up next to the ruins, but what is left of the old Cathedral still stands, an empty shell, open to the sky, with its broken and scarred walls. The altar is still there with replicas of the original Charred Cross and Cross of Nails.

The old Cathedral, empty, open, broken, and scarred is transformed into a place of dignity and peace by the power of the Holy Spirit working through the hearts and minds of the people of Coventry.

Right Here In My Church

April McClure Stewart

He has shown strength with his arm; he has scat-
tered the proud in the thoughts of their hearts. He
has brought down the powerful from their thrones
and lifted up the lowly. (vv. 51-52)

I first met Brayden when he was nine years old. He was a
fourth grader at the elementary school across the street from the
church. The minute he appeared in my Bible study class at the
mid-week program we had at the church, I branded him "trouble-
maker." Within thirty seconds of entering the room he had pulled
a chair out from under a girl, punched the only other boy in the
class in the arm, and used a four-letter word that was definitely not
appropriate for church.

After the Bible study, I pulled aside the minister and asked her
for the details about Brayden. His father was in jail for the third
time. His mother had abused him and was not allowed to see him.
He was living with a grandmother who worked second shift and
the woman who provided him childcare was not available until
6:00 p.m. The reason he was in our program was because the prin-
cipal at the grade school, an occasional attender of the church, had
heard that our program did not finish until 7:30. That meant that at
least one night a week, Brayden would not be on his own for three
hours, getting into trouble.

It was not an easy thing to have Brayden in class. He was
constantly changing the subject to talk about things that he had
heard about girls from his twenty-year-old uncle — hardly the
type of things we would normally be discussing in class; or he
would tell stories he had heard about his father. He was also antsy.
He liked to move around and he liked to bother the girls. He especially liked to bother the girls by moving them — seizing their

20

chairs and hurling them to the ground. To combat this problem, Brayden sat right next to me, and I had him do things like help with passing out papers when he behaved himself. We also devised a system where he would go stand by the door if he felt himself getting angry. That worked some of the time, but many times he would get angry anyway, and when that happened he would call other people names, insult them as badly as he could, and it would always end with him, and at least one more child, crying. I resented him for it.

My Bible study was not the only time that Brayden acted up. In recreation he would hit and pinch people. During music, he goofed around and carried on conversations entirely separate from the task at hand. During mealtime, he was an absolute terror, throwing food, spitting at people, and making the little kids cry. Our program team had what seemed like weekly meetings about him, and didn't know what to do. We tried talking to him, calling his grandmother, asking for volunteers to accompany him at all times. We tried to explain what "church" behavior was and we put up "no running" signs in that hallway. We had lengthy discussions in our Bible study about what subjects were and were not appropriate in church. As a team, we adults rolled our eyes, sighed, and moaned about having to accommodate Brayden. I think we all secretly hoped his grandmother would take him to another babysitter or that he would not come back the next Wednesday. I know I did.

But there was no such luck for us. The rest of the kids missed an occasional Wednesday. Some got sick, some had other things to do every once in a while, but not Brayden. He was there every single Wednesday, and he was always at the same energy level — extremely high. As time went by, I became more and more frustrated. It seemed that I was always correcting and disciplining Brayden, and quite frankly, I wanted the whole thing to go away.

Sometime in March, after about seven months of meeting every Wednesday, Brayden started giving me a hug when he left for the evening with his babysitter. One day, I saw him in the grocery store, and he ran up to me and pulled me over to meet his grandmother, who was one of the cashiers. He bragged, "This is my teacher at my church." I told the minister about it and she reported

21

that the same thing happened to her. Another woman, who was his substitute teacher at the grade school, reported that Brayden had introduced her to the class on a day she subbed saying, "Mrs. Andrews goes to my church with me on Wednesday nights."

One day, toward the end of the school year, we were discussing hospitality in class. I asked the kids to think about a place where they felt most secure — most at home. Some said their bedrooms, or outside at their houses. One kid said the playroom at his grandpa's house. When it came to Brayden, he said, "Man, I've lived in a million places." We all laughed and waited for him to go on. "You mean the place where we feel happy and safe?" he asked, and I said, "Yes." "Oh," he said, matter-of-factly, "that's right here in my church."

Right here in his church. Right here in *my* church. Right here where I had not wanted him to be.

Gram

William Bell

> ... an angel of the Lord appeared to him in a dream
> and said, "Joseph, son of David, do not be afraid
> to take Mary as your wife, for the child conceived
> in her is from the Holy Spirit. She will bear a son,
> and you are to name him Jesus...." (vv. 20b-21a)

Cecelia, my paternal grandmother, died in the late fall of 1969, shortly after I began my military assignment in what was then known as the Republic of South Vietnam. Because I was in-country for such a short period of time, it was determined that I would not be allowed to attend the funeral services. I was both saddened and disappointed at this decision, for I was particularly close to "Gram," as I called her, not only because our family lived in her home until I was about seven, but also because I greatly admired her. Losing her husband, my grandfather, shortly after my father was born, Gram was forced to go to work, and for much of her working life, performed housekeeping services for her local parish and school. When Gram retired after more than thirty years of service, she received thirty silver dollars as her retirement pension. I remember thinking how unfair thirty silver dollars were after a lifetime of hard work, particularly considering the physical toll it took on Gram's hands, back, etc., but Gram was proud of her "reward" nonetheless. And I was proud of her as well.

Besides being hardworking, Gram played piano and loved ragtime music, and of course her beloved Detroit Tigers. The Tigers won the series in 1968, and Gram was very optimistic that they would repeat. Gram was very intelligent, and I remember fondly our discussions of current events and politics. She was very opinionated. After receiving the news of Gram's death, I remembered those discussions (some were very spirited) and I realized just how much I was going to miss her.

I received Gram's last letter after the news of her death. She wrote often while I was in the service, and I was always amazed at how legible her letters were, given her poor eyesight; how insightful and upbeat. In her last letter she wrote that she was very optimistic that our new President, Richard Nixon, was going to end the war, and I would be home soon. As a life-long Democrat, this letter could not have been easy for Gram to pen, for she was not in favor of the Vietnam conflict. I remember thinking that this letter was the last time I would be hearing from Gram, but little did I know that she wasn't quite finished communicating with me.

A few months after Gram's death, while I was still in Vietnam, I was stricken with what then was diagnosed as malaria. Accompanying this malady was high fever, and I remember having what has been commonly referred to as the "near-death" experience. My experience included hovering over, and being able to see what appeared to be my sleeping body. Then, quite to my surprise, I was visited by my recently-deceased grandmother. Interestingly enough, Gram appeared to be about twenty years younger, but was dressed in her favorite red and white checkerboard dress. She told me not be frightened, that I was going to recover. She also mentioned that she was wrong, and the Vietnam conflict was not going to end soon, but I would be safe, and needed to be careful at all times. I trusted my grandmother, and her reassuring words that I would survive Vietnam went a long way to alleviate my fears.

Gram has visited me several times since my Vietnam encounter. On these occasions she appeared while I was asleep. On two such occasions that I recall vividly, she appeared just prior to the birth of each of our sons, Ian and Matthew. My wife, Margaret, and I decided to forgo knowing the sex of each child, but Gram informed me in advance. Again, I was startled by her predictive revelations, and her ostensible knowledge of the future. She was very pleased with both boys, and told me they were great kids.

Gram has, I think, attempted to visit with me on several other occasions, but I was unable to make contact. I can only hope that

Gram keeps trying to visit with me, and that I have an opportunity to tell her that I miss her and hope she is doing well. I must admit I am curious about Gram's afterlife experiences, and would love to discuss them with her. Knowing Gram, I am sure it would turn into a "spirited" discussion.

Christmas

I like imaging the shepherds gazing at the stars in the night sky as they kept watch over their sheep. I love to lie on the ground at night and watch the wonder, immensity, and dance of the night sky. I find the story of the angels appearing and speaking to the Shepherds irresistible. I admit that an angel or two has spoken to me.

Esther Armstrong

Esther Armstrong, *Journey Into Freedom* newsletter, 40th edition. Portland, Oregon, October, 2003, p. 3.

Christmas Presence

Janice Hammerquist

The people who walked in darkness have seen a
great light: those who lived in a land of deep dark-
ness — on them light has shined. (v. 2)

When my dad passed away unexpectedly, we were shocked, saddened, and overwhelmed. He had been caring for my mother, who was an invalid suffering from emphysema, and we had to hastily decide how to care for her and get her medication figured out. It was a difficult time, as these things always are. We did find a lady to stay with mother so that she could stay at home, rather than go into a nursing home. My dad died in July, and on Christmas Eve, I had gone to stay with my mother so that her caretaker could have Christmas off. My own family was at home celebrating Christmas. I had to leave the festivities at home to spend the night with my mother. As I was sitting there with her, I was down in the dumps, feeling sorry for myself, missing my family, and especially, missing my dad. Suddenly, without any warning, I felt his presence in the room. I didn't see him, as much as feel he was there. He was happy — I think even laughing, and somehow conveyed to me that all was well. It was very fleeting to me, but very real, and I immediately felt much better. That short moment will always be with me, and it gives me comfort still, as it did sixteen years ago.

Warnings

Now after they had left, an angel of the Lord appeared to Joseph in a dream and said, "Get up, take the child and his mother, and flee to Egypt, and remain there until I tell you...." When Herod died, an angel of the Lord suddenly appeared in a dream to Joseph in Egypt and said, "Get up, take the child and his mother, and go to the land of Israel, for those who were seeking the child's life are dead." (vv. 13a, 19-20)

Vickie Eckoldt

My first experience with a vision was when I was fourteen years old. The telephone rang and as my mother was walking across the room to answer it, I had this vision of my great-aunt and knew she had passed away. Before my mother answered the phone, I told her her that her aunt had passed away. After listening to her conversation, I knew I was right. When she hung up the phone she turned to me and said, "How did you know that? She hasn't even been sick. What made you say that?" All I could say to her was that I just knew it.

On another occasion, while packing up the car for our trip to Tennessee, I had a vision of a multiple-car accident on the freeway. I then realized that if we left at this time our car could be involved in that accident. I was sure we would not return home if we left at this time. I told my husband and daughter of my vision and felt that we should wait until morning. Knowing of other visions I have had that were so accurate, they agreed we should wait. That night, on the 10:00 news, there was a story about a multiple-car accident, just as I had seen it.

Elaine Klemm Grau

My heart was heavy and tears came easily. It was three months after I had been dismissed from a pastoral assistant program at the local seminary. I knew that God had called me to this in a dream, and after two years and 27 credits, I was asked to leave. I was assured that I had not done anything wrong and I was crushed that I never really knew the reason for my dismissal from the program. I assumed that it was because I was in my mid-seventies, but they did not want to tell me this. Once again, I slipped into contemplative prayer to listen for his voice and to discern the path he wanted me to follow. Deep in prayer, I suddenly saw a white oval light, and in it was a beautiful child with golden brown curls and a child's face lovelier than any I had ever seen before! He had high cheekbones and a flawless bronze complexion. He was dressed in a plain white garment with a gold cross in the center. His lovely brown eyes were brimming with tears as he held his arms out to me. I do not know how long the vision lasted — time seemed absent from the event. He then vanished in the shimmering light. I emerged from my prayer peaceful and serene, and knowing my direction.

That afternoon, I telephoned another seminary and inquired about their program. It was there I began a course in spiritual direction, and that is what I practice today. My love of God has deepened with each passing day and his image remains imbedded in my mind and heart.

A Dog Came For Christmas

John Sumwalt

And the Word became flesh and lived among us,
and we have seen his glory.... (v. 14)

There was once an old man who did not have a dog. He did not have a wife (she had died the Christmas before). He did not have any family or friends to speak of; he did not have anything to fill the emptiness that sat like a dead weight on his heart.

Neighbors and people from the church had come by in the weeks and months after Margaret had died, but he had turned them away with polite lies, saying he was doing all right, that he was keeping busy, and, no, there was nothing they could do for him.

Each time he closed the door on one of these offers of kindness, the old man felt older and smaller. He had barely enough energy to pull himself up from the table after his meals and walk outside to the front stoop, where he sat for hours on end, day after day.

It was late in the afternoon of one of these long vigils, just before dusk, in the twilight moment when the last rays of sunlight fade into darkness, that the old man first became aware of the dog's presence. He appeared as a white blur from behind a bush at the end of the street.

As the dog drew near, he sank to the ground, creeping carefully on his belly as if stalking some kind of prey. He stopped about three feet from the old man's right foot.

The old man tried to shoo him away. "Get out of here! Go home! It's supper time; you're not going to get anything here."

It was the same every day after that. The dog appeared late in the afternoon, and each time the old man tried to chase him away. Every day the dog came closer and closer, till one day, without a word, the old man let him stay. The two sat together for over an hour. Then, suddenly, the dog made his move, slowly sliding forward, inch by inch, until his nose rested on the old man's foot.

The next morning, the old man rose early and hurried through breakfast. He quickly washed the dishes and straightened the house. Then he got into the car and drove to Wal-Mart. The store was crowded with last-minute Christmas Eve shoppers. The old man grabbed a cart and filled it with bags of rawhide bones, a couple of soft rubber balls, the biggest bag of dog food he could find, several dog toys that jingled and jangled, and one of those huge, comfy doggie pillow beds. He threw it all in the car, stopped on the way home to pick up the Christmas tree, took everything into the house, decorated the tree, wrapped the presents, and still managed to be sitting in his chair on the stoop when the dog appeared at the usual time.

The dog came straight to the old man and lay down at his feet. The old man leaned over and patted him on the head. "How are you, fella? It's good to see you." The dog rolled over on his back, with all four feet in the air, and the old man reached down and scratched his belly.

After a while, the old man got up and walked to the door. Holding it open wide, he looked at the dog and said, "Well, what are you waiting for? Get in here. It's time for our supper."

Epiphany

... at certain times we may experience an epiphany, a sudden illumination of our intimate union with the Divine. During an epiphany, your relationship to God is transformed from one of doubt or fear into one of deep trust.

Caroline Myss

Caroline Myss, *Sacred Contracts: Awakening Your Divine Potential* (Three Rivers, Michigan: Three Rivers Press, 2003), p. 27.

Metacosmic Light

Gail C. Ingle

*For darkness shall cover the earth, and thick dark-
ness the peoples; but the Lord will arise upon you,
and his glory will appear over you.* (v. 2)

I have been interested in spiritual matters for a long time. On
May 19, 1989, I had a spiritual experience that I will never forget.
I was at my friends' home to participate in a prayer/healing circle.
We were all standing in a darkened room lit only with candles. My
arms felt weightless and they involuntarily began to rise until they
were above my head. Suddenly, I felt something like a bolt of light-
ning enter my head and go through my body. I began to cry. My
friends asked me if I was all right and I nodded silently. They told
me they could see the colors violet and green surrounding me. I
must have stood there for about five minutes with my arms straight
up in the air before they slowly returned to my side. I felt extremely peaceful long into the night. When I got home, I sat down
and wrote the poem, "Metacosmic Light."

Metacosmic Light
*Little, white candles flicker,
As the smooth, pink crystals glow.
My arms lose all their feeling
When the energy starts to flow.
My wrists are pulled by magnets,
The force too much to bear;
I raise my arms to heaven
To seek the mystery there.
My hands stretch out and upward,
Stretch as far as they will go.*

37

The light comes crashing through me
Like an arrow from a bow.
As the tears flow down my cheeks,
Friends are reaching out to me,
But I want nothing from them,
So they step back graciously.
When all the light has pierced my brain,
My arms shine violet and green.
My friends applaud my courage,
Delighted by what they've seen.
Now, my arms, demagnetized,
Fall silently to my side.
The warmth of love surrounds me,
For a part of me has died.
The little white candles burn down
Though the crystals will always glow.
My heart is full of loving.
My life has begun to grow.

May 19, 1989

Editor's Note: My sister-in-law, Linda, phoned in early June of 2004 to tell me that her co-worker and friend, Gail Ingle, was near death in a nearby hospital and had mentioned she would like to meet me. I went the next day, because Gail is the contributor of two marvelous personal stories to the *Visions* series and I was eager to meet her. Linda told me that Gail was at peace and full of love and light. She was right. I have never met anyone about to pass over who was so full of joy. Gail blessed me immediately with a warm smile. She thanked me for the opportunity to publish her stories. I told her what a blessing her brave witness has been to the many, many souls who have already read her "Dreams" story in *Sharing Visions*, and will soon read "Metacosmic Light," in this volume.

Gail passed on June 13. We celebrated her life on a perfect summer evening, at her church in Genesee, a beautiful country village in southeast Wisconsin. Gail's family and friends told of

38

her great love for all of the people who crossed her path. One of her colleagues at Waukesha South High School, where Gail taught for over twenty years, related how much she was loved by her students, how many graduates would return with their children to introduce them to their favorite teacher. I give thanks to God for a shining life.

Your Dad Likes You

Kathleen A. "Kit" Slawski

And when Jesus had been baptized, just as he came up from the water, suddenly the heavens were opened to him and he saw the Spirit of God descending like a dove and alighting on him. And a voice from heaven said, "This is my Son, the Beloved, with whom I am well pleased." (vv. 16-17)

My favorite memory will always be the special way the *Peanuts* characters helped my father celebrate his daughters' thirteenth birthdays. In the strip appearing on October 4, 1970, Peppermint Patty called Charlie Brown over to her house to show him what her father had given her for her birthday. Charlie Brown admired the roses, and Peppermint Patty said, "He said that I'm growing up fast and soon I'll be a beautiful young lady and all the boys will be calling me up so he just wanted to be the first one in my life to give me a dozen roses! He calls me a 'rare gem.' " Charlie Brown replied, "Your dad likes you ... happy birthday...."

My father, Matt Wey, saved that comic strip. On my thirteenth birthday, I received from my father one dozen beautiful red roses and a statuette of Peppermint Patty that read, "To my Rare Gem." When my two younger sisters, Eileen and Molly, reached their thirteenth birthdays, they too were honored with this special *Peanuts* treat from our father.

Thank you, Charles Schulz, for this and many more special memories!

An Unexpected Song

Derrick Sanderson

*The Lord called me before I was born, while I was
in my mother's womb he named me.*
— Isaiah 49:1b

*He drew me up from the desolate pit, out of the
miry bog, and set my feet upon a rock, making my
steps secure. He put a new song in my mouth, a
song of praise to our God. Many will see and fear,
and put their trust in the Lord.*   — Psalm 40:2-3

Deep down, I have always known that God has been in my
life, but I am a very independent person and I find it hard to listen
to God's will — especially when things aren't going the way that
I planned them. Fortunately for me, God knows this. When the
time comes that I need to receive his message, he lets me know in
a way that I cannot miss. Without God's intervention I know that I
would not be alive today.

The problems began with my relationship with my father, or I
should say, lack thereof. My parents got divorced when I was two
and my father decided to move to southern California, separating
himself from my brother and me by 2,800 miles. His visits were
few and far between, leaving all of my parental guidance in the
hands of my mother. My brother tried his best to be a father figure
in my life by teaching me how to ride a bike and things of that
nature, but he was too young to truly be the kind of parental figure
that I needed and craved as a very strong-willed child.

As I got older, I started to think of my father in terms of what
I needed and wanted. Like any young boy, I wanted my father to
be at my soccer games. I wanted him to take me out fishing. I
wanted to feel his love and compassion. In short, I wanted him to

41

be there for me day in and day out. My father had always told me that he would be there for me, but there was only one time in my life when he actually was. The love-hate relationship that many sons have with their fathers quickly grew into a hate-only relationship for me. I hated him for all of the times that he said he would be there for me and then hung up the phone and went about his life. I hated him for missing my childhood. I hated him for not disciplining me when I caused problems. Most of all, I hated it when he said that he loved me.

It was at the peak of this hatred, during my teen years, that my father was struck a crucial blow: he was diagnosed with Progressive Supranuclear Palsey, or PSP. PSP is an incurable disease and the symptoms are untreatable. That meant that not only was he going to die from this disease, he was going to die painfully of its side effects. Unfortunately, the life expectancy is unknown with this disease because it affects everyone individually and because many of the PSP victims die of the symptoms rather than the disease. My father's condition seemed at first to be progressing slowly, starting with some difficulty eating food and loss of voluntary eye movement. However, his condition became exponentially worse in a rather short period of time, forcing my father to move into an assisted living community.

I had seen my father only twice in the previous two years and I decided that, since his condition was worsening rapidly, I would go visit him over my Thanksgiving break from school. I flew out to California and stayed at the house with my stepmom. Because of my father's condition, and because he was living in the assisted living community, I only got to spend a short amount of time with him. It was depressingly apparent, however, that the strong man I once knew no longer existed. All that was left was a withered, hunched-over, middle-aged man on the brink of defeat.

One night, we both decided to get a professional massage to relieve my father of some of the muscle tension that PSP caused. I didn't think anything negative would come out of the experience, but I was wrong. At the spa, I had to help my dad undress and get onto the massage table in a semi-comfortable position so that he could get his massage. I left the room to the sound of my father moaning in discomfort and embarrassment that he could not longer do these things on his own.

My own massage relaxed my mind and body and helped me forget what I had just witnessed and the distance that had grown between us. Then as I lay half sleeping on the table, a knock came at the door. My father's masseuse entered and told me that his massage was done and that he needed help getting dressed. I hurriedly put on my clothes and went to help him. As I entered the room, he was struggling desperately to right himself. I quickly but tenderly helped him sit up. Even this simple motion caused him a great amount of discomfort. I helped him dress, and as I was putting on his shoes he said, "Why did this happen to me? I hate this." I could say nothing other than, "I know, Dad, I know."

Time went on and I became more and more disgusted with myself. No matter how hard I tried, I could not forgive my father for what he had — or had not — done to me. By early spring of the next year, the PSP had greatly weakened his immune system, leaving him victim to a lung infection. Normally, such an infection wouldn't be a big deal, but because of his state, he had to be admitted to the hospital.

My stepmom did a great job of keeping us updated on his condition. She relayed the doctor's thoughts on my father's condition: He should recover shortly with the help of an air tube. Within a week or two, my father was doing much better and was looking forward to being released from the hospital. However, once the air tube was removed, the infection quickly took hold again, forcing him to stay in the hospital. Sensing that his days might be numbered, my brother and I decided to go and visit. I had a three-day weekend coming up a couple of weeks later, and I decided that we should go then.

Three days later, I was taken out of my second period class and my mother told me my father had died the night before. I sat in silence as they told me that, late the night before; he had painfully pulled the air tube out of his esophagus. They told me that he hadn't made a sound, despite ripping everything from his lungs into his mouth, and that he had died quickly once off the machine. I was in disbelief at first because that was not the man I knew: My

43

father never gave up. But I realized that he hadn't given up, he simply couldn't handle being sick anymore or causing pain and sorrow to his loved ones.

Before he died, he had decided that he wanted to be buried in Marshall, Wisconsin, on the family farm. As I lowered his ashes into the ground, a hatred for myself started to stir within me. As the days passed after the funeral, I sank deeper and deeper into depression and began to feel more and more helpless and alone. I utterly hated myself and my life. I had tried to live my father's dying days according to my own schedule. I had failed to acknowledge that his situation was a bigger issue than my own life, and I couldn't handle that realization. I denounced God, claiming that he couldn't be all good if he could do this to me.

My strong independence kept me from seeking help from my family, friends, counselors, and especially God. Even when gestures were made, I wouldn't let anyone help me. As my hatred grew, so did the feeling that I was a waste of space. I began to think that life would be much better without me. Suicide became more and more appealing each day. I never considered it seriously until I reached the point when I couldn't handle it anymore, and I decided that I was going to kill myself. When I got home from school, I locked myself in the bathroom and held a razor blade to my wrist. I took one last look into the mirror and said to myself, "Good-bye, I'm sorry." But something inside kept me from making the cut. I couldn't bear to make my family feel the way I had felt after my father took away the chance for me to say good-bye. I didn't want to go like that, at least not at this time. So I pulled through the rest of my senior year in high school, hating every moment of my worthless existence, especially time spent around extended family.

A blessing was waiting for me in the form of an invitation to be a counselor at a United Methodist youth summer church camp called YOMICA. I'm not completely sure why I accepted the invitation, but I thought hanging out with kids for a week would be a nice escape from my life. I was a little uncomfortable with the decision, seeing that I didn't think God was good, but since the

44

camp was fast approaching, I figured it was unfair of me to back out and I felt obligated to give it a shot.

Camp started, and I felt awkwardly out of place. I was singing and praying about how God was good and how he could heal our pain, but I *didn't believe* he was good and I thought he was *the cause* of my pain. To say the least, I was simply going through the motions. But then the greatest moment of my life occurred.

It was a warm July night, and I was sitting with my campers in the amphitheater-style chapel overlooking the lake that bordered the camp, trying to avoid as much of the devotion as possible. I paused from singing and noticed how brightly the moon was shining upon the log cross. It was, at that point, much brighter than when we had begun the devotion. I looked around to see if anyone else noticed it, but everyone was too involved in the service. I took a moment and looked up at the sky and said, "God, I don't know what is going on in my life, but I've had enough of this." As my eyes focused back on the cross, the children's singing cut back into my consciousness with, "Father, I adore you, and I'll lay my life before you. How I love you." At that moment my heart swelled, and the air painfully escaped my lungs and I heard, "Be still and know that I am God; set me as a seal upon your heart." Now, I'm not claiming that God was actually talking to me, because I don't really know how that works. But, from somewhere inside of me, I heard — or better yet, felt — that message. As I struggled for air, I couldn't focus on anything but that moonlit cross. My mind thought about nothing but the glorious song of those beautiful children. For the first time in my life I was at peace, and for the first time in a long time, I was truly happy. I was happy to be alive and thankful for God's message.

Editor's Note: Derrick's shining moment occurred the summer of 2002 at Pine Lake United Methodist Camp, Westfield, Wisconsin.

A Dog's Life

David Michael Smith

One thing I ask of the Lord, the will I seek after:
to live in the house of the Lord all the days of my
life.... (v. 4a)

The phone rang at precisely 9 p.m. as a drought buster of a storm raged angrily outside our bedroom windows. Instinctively, my wife and I both knew who it was and I answered the call with a dull numbness, as if I'd been maced with Novocain.

"Mr. Smith, this is John at the veterinary hospital," the voice flatly reported in a grave monotone. "I'm afraid things have taken a turn for the worse." My heart sank and tears spilled from my wife's eyes behind me. She could tell from my wooden expression that the news wasn't good.

"I'd like your permission to do some emergency exploratory surgery, see if there's anything I can do to save your dog, Brandy. It's a long shot, but our only hope."

I paused, knowing there was more.

"But if I can't do anything, I'll need to put her down," he added with a solemn whisper. "It's the humane thing to do. She's very sick and suffering."

I felt like someone sucker punched me in the gut. I couldn't breathe.

"I need to discuss this with my wife, please, John," I managed, my voice shaky. "I'll call you right back."

I hung up and discussed the matter with my wife. We both agreed that we wanted to be there for our friend, for our *child*, to provide a comforting and familiar presence. For years we had tried to start a family with no success. Everything was tried during those tedious months, every imaginable process and method and wive's tale and suggestion, not to mention countless prayers of faith. But it was not meant to be; some things just aren't. Each effort fell short, and our marriage, though strengthened by the experiences, remained childless.

This dog was more than a pet to us; she was a precious jewel in our daily lives, a member of our family. She was a faithful companion, lovable, loyal, and humorous. We made the hard decision while wiping away tears, the humane decision, to bypass the surgery and go over in the evening rainstorm. We would hold our dear pet, Brandy, as she was given the needles that would help her to pass over to the eternal side of existence.

I called back to inform the doctor of our decision. Strangely, it took John five rings to answer his cell phone, despite knowing I was calling right back. He told me he'd have the phone by his side. Finally, the call was accepted with an echoing click.

"Mr. Smith," the voice hesitated with great emotion, "your dog just collapsed into my arms. Oh, God, I think she's dying...." He fumbled with his stethoscope on the other end while I listened to the surrealistic nightmare in my ear, wishing I would wake up. "Oh, God, I'm so sorry ... she just took her last breath. She's gone." The man was in tears. I soon joined him, sobbing like a newborn.

Our drive over to the vet's office was a silent one until my wife suggested we relive special memories. There were many, and we found ourselves laughing, and then crying all over again. Brandy had impacted our lives more than we realized.

Inside the doctor's office, abandoned and quiet on a Sunday night, we thanked John for being there to hold our friend as she passed away. It was more than sheer coincidence that he happened to be there. Moments later, our hearts were warmed when we saw her still, furry body. She was clearly at peace, as if she were merely sleeping.

After wrapping Brandy in cotton blankets, we laid her gently onto the backseat of our car. Wet and still in shock, we slowly backed out and exited the parking lot with a reverent spirit.

About a mile or two later, my wife broke the solitude with a loud, startled scream. I quickly asked her, "What's wrong?"

"Brandy just licked me! On the back of my neck! Honestly, I felt it!" My wife was ecstatic, thrilled beyond words.

I peered into the backseat, half expecting a modern day Lazarus miracle, but, of course, the dog remained very much still and wrapped in blankets.

"Maybe you just felt something, Honey, a wisp of air or something," I offered, confused yet intrigued.

"No, it was her, I know it was her," she insisted, assured of what occurred. "That dog has given me so many kisses over the years; it was exactly the same. I know it was her."

For several long moments silence returned to the compartment of our vehicle. Only the rhythmic reverberation of wipers working to clear raindrops from the windshield was audible.

"Brandy wanted to let us know she's okay," my wife explained, breaking the quietness. "I bet that's why she licked me. To let us know that she's fine, that she's moved on, and waiting for us." The event comforted our mourning hearts, and softened our sorrow.

The next morning we buried our precious *daughter* as it lightly misted from the dreary, carbonized skies. We read liturgy from the *Episcopal Prayer Book* and offered prayers for her soul. We gave thanks for her thirteen years with us, each one good, happy, and healthy. I placed a University of Tennessee Volunteers baseball cap on her furry head, one I often wore on cold mornings as we walked together in the woods, before closing the box for the final time. My wife also added several of the dog's favorite treats, and all of her play balls. There were many. Even during her last days the dog played with those balls with the energy of a puppy.

The next evening our kindly church priest called to check in, having heard the news of our loss. We discussed animals and souls and heaven mostly. He assured me that the perfection of God's holy landscape would be dotted with all kinds of creatures, especially pets. If God cared enough to make it, he would surely care enough to desire it in his heavenly kingdom. But this I already knew. For on the rainy, dark night our dog left us, she also left a sign that she was still very much alive, a wet lick across my wife's neck, a canine kiss, from the golden retriever we knew as Brandy.

A Comforting Dream

Harold Klug

Blessed are those who mourn, for they will be comforted. (v. 4)

My healing vision from God came in a dream.

Many years ago, I had my tractor hitched onto a new Case corn shredder and wanted to see how it worked. So, I decided to try it out in the orchard, where the grass was about three feet high. My little four-year-old daughter wanted to sit on the tractor with me, but I told her she couldn't go along. She followed without my noticing. I ran her over, and she died in my arms as I carried her to the house.

At the funeral, I could not stand at the coffin as people came up to grieve with me. I was so devastated that I cried every day for a full year. Then, I believe, the Lord decided I had grieved enough. The Lord is sometimes slow to heal, but he is very dependable.

I dreamed one night that I went into a cemetery that was underground. The caretaker asked if I would like to see my father. I said "Yes," and he pulled a slab out from the wall, and there lay my departed father. The caretaker then asked if I would like to see my daughter. I said that I would, so he took me to a little creek, and there she was, picking flowers and happy.

This vision ended my life of grieving. I thought I would never laugh or smile again, but God showed me that all is well in his care.

My daughter, Linda, was the first to be buried from St. Paul's Lutheran Church in Random Lake, Wisconsin. We had just finished building it, and I was the head of the building committee. It still brings tears to my eyes to tell this tragic story, but the whole, horrible experience made a better person out of me.

The Horse Whisperer

William Lee Rand

*Now we have received not the spirit of the world,
but the Spirit that is from God, so that we may
understand the gifts bestowed on us by God. And
we speak of these things in words not taught by
human wisdom but taught by the Spirit, interpret-
ing spiritual things to those who are spiritual.*
(vv. 12-13)

While on Maui last May, I had the good fortune to attend a
Horse Whisperer training session led by Franklin Levinson. Many
of his methods are based on those used in the movie of the same
name, starring Robert Redford.

According to Franklin, there are two ways we can interact with
a horse. One is through force (i.e., fear-based control); the other,
to lead it through trust, respect, knowledge, and mutual agreement
(i.e., love). The first way produces a slave, a being whose actions
are motivated by fear of punishment, a captive. The other way
produces a willing partner, a loyal and trusted friend, and a relationship built on respect.

Franklin teaches students how to communicate and interact
with horses on a primal level, to connect directly with a horse's
psyche and instincts. Horses are amazingly sensitive, intelligent,
and aware. Being herd animals, they have a highly developed ability
to understand and respond to a leader. (We also found they are
amazingly telepathic and are healers.) With this understanding,
it's possible to get horses to do whatever you want them to do —
within reason — if you first gain their trust and show them you are
worthy of being their leader.

We were shown several body movements and postures horses
use to communicate various feelings and ideas. For example, if a

horse likes you, it will show affection by placing its head on your chest. If it likes what you're doing and is receptive to it, it will lower its head and blow through its lips. We were shown how to become friends by focusing on feelings of peace and love — which the horse can feel — and by petting and scratching the horse. Once trust is formed, the horse will want to be near you; so if you begin walking around the corral, the horse will follow. Doing this establishes you as the leader. Then by using a wand and standing in the center of the corral and simply holding it up off to your side, the horse will begin running around the outside of the corral. If you lower the wand, the horse will stop and walk back to you.

One of the horses we worked with was named Dukie. We were able to get him to jump over a short barrier as he ran around the corral. We found that the clearer your expectation and the stronger your energy about this, the better rapport you had with the horse and the more responsive it would become. When doing this, I felt a definite feeling of partnership and shared love, that Dukie was doing what I wanted because he truly enjoyed doing so.

After each student interacted with the horse in this way, Franklin had us do something that produced an amazing result. When it was each person's turn, Franklin asked him or her to close their eyes and tell what was seen or felt. Many would start crying and say that the horse was healing some emotional wound they had from childhood or other experiences.

When it was my turn, I began doing Reiki* on Dukie, and he immediately took on a different posture, which Franklin noticed. He placed his head down in a receptive posture, and Franklin said the horse really liked what I was doing. Then, after this, he asked me to place my arms on the corral bar and not pay any attention to Dukie. When I did this, Dukie came up behind me and began nuzzling me on the back around my heart in a very gentle and affectionate way. Then he began nibbling on my ear with his lips. This felt both unusual and wonderful.

Then I was asked to go inward and tell what I saw. Dukie began to place an image in my mind that was more than just an image. The horse was running through a field of grass, and the sun was shining a glorious, warm, golden light. The horse was filled

51

with a sense of being one with nature and filled with great joy — the joy of life and the joy of being free. Then I felt Dukie ask if I would like to join him, and as soon as I said yes, I was there with him, bathed in the energy and connected with all the forces of nature and feeling so free. This was very moving, and I feel that it was Dukie's way of thanking me for the Reiki* I had shared with him.

Later, after we left and were on the beach watching windsurfers, Dukie came to me inwardly and again nuzzled the back of my heart. Then he began working with my solar plexus energy. There were some stuck negative feelings and energies there that I had been dealing with and working to heal, but hadn't been able to do so. I felt the blocks melting and releasing, and they were gone. This was another amazing experience and a real miracle.

I'm blessed to have spent this healing time with Dukie, merging with his consciousness and feeling what he feels; noble, mystical feelings of grace, strength, loyalty, emotional clarity, love, and a willingness to help. I learned so much about being a healer and the potential within all living beings.

*Reiki is a method of natural healing based on the application of "Universal Life Force Energy."

An Old Enemy

Kendall W. Anderson

So when you are offering your gift at the altar, if you remember that your brother or sister has something against you, leave your gift there before the altar and go; first be reconciled with your brother or sister, and then come and offer your gift. (vv. 23-24)

We met on a commercial flight between Minneapolis and Detroit sometime in the late 1950s. He was Asian. It was almost fifteen years after the war. I don't remember his name, but I still have his business card somewhere in my desk. I'm not sure why I sat beside him. In those days the airlines still allowed you to pick your own seat. I could have sat with any number of people, or I could have sat by myself. For some reason, I chose to sit beside him.

The plane took off, and after we had been flying for a little while, I asked him if he was Japanese. He said, "Yes." On an impulse I decided to tell him a story that I had just heard — about a man who died and was given the option of going to heaven or hell. He decided to go to hell because he thought that was where his friends were most likely to be. When he arrived in hell he discovered that there was plenty of rice and other good things to eat, but everyone was starving because the chopsticks were all six feet long. He didn't like the looks of things in hell, so he asked if he could go to heaven instead. He was given permission to go and when he arrived he discovered that everything was exactly the same, except in heaven they were feeding each other.

"Oh," said my companion, "you must be a Christian. I am, too."

He went on to tell that his mother was a Christian and that he had become a Christian after the war. I asked him what he had done during the war. He said that he had been a fighter pilot in the Southwest Pacific. I told him that I had been a fighter pilot, too, in the same area. We quickly compared notes and discovered that we had flown missions over Formosa at the same time. Neither of us said it aloud, but I'm sure it occurred to him, as is did to me, that had we met in the air during the war, we would have tried to kill each other.

We went on to talk about our work. He was serving on the economic council of the United Nations as a representative of Japan. I thought about the great number of people throughout the world that he was able to help with his work, and me with mine, and it struck me what a great tragedy it would have been if one of us had killed the other.

When I got off the plane, I didn't hate the Japanese people anymore, and I knew the meaning of forgiveness.

Editor's Note: Kendall W. Anderson related this account of his unexpected meeting with his old enemy to the editor in September of 1990. Ken served as a fighter pilot with the 39th Fighter Squadron in the Southwest Pacific in World War II. He is a graduate of Bangor Theological Seminary and served pastorates in New England and Wisconsin before retiring in 1984. "An Old Enemy" appeared in *Lectionary Stories,* by John Sumwalt, CSS Publishing Company, Inc, 1991, pp. 27-28.

Discerning God's Direction

Jane Moschenrose

According to the grace of God given to me, like a skilled master builder I laid a foundation, and someone else is building on it. Each builder must choose with care how to build on it ... Do not deceive yourselves. If you think that you are wise in this age, you should become fools so that you may become wise. For the wisdom of this world is foolishness with God ... So let not one boast about human leaders.... (vv. 10, 18-19a, 21a)

Our church of 100 active members was in a dilemma. We had sold our large building years ago, because its maintenance had demanded far too much of our energy and financial resources. If we remained in the office space we had rented for the past six years, we would be financially solvent, but unable to do much ministry during the week. We rarely had visitors in worship, because it was difficult to find our rented space, and frankly, we rarely invited our friends to church because we were embarrassed that our worship space didn't feel or look like a sanctuary.

Our realtor had spent two years searching for either an existing building, or property, on which to build a new facility, and everything available was either too expensive, or in an area that wasn't geographically central for the majority of our current membership.

Finally the realtor found a piece of property that met our needs. The church leadership quickly made an offer, while securing a 120 day "due diligence" period in which to decide whether or not to go through with the purchase. We spent these months in much prayer and discussion. We all agreed on two things — the location was perfect, but the price tag was not. There was no way we could both buy the property *and* build a church (at least, one that was larger than a small house) within the next five years and still maintain the conservative financial strategies we had used up to this point. If we stayed where we were, we would die as the membership died or left the church. If we risked everything we had financially, bought the property, and put a church building on it, we would have about four years to double in membership and financial giving before going broke. Either decision held major risks, though the former was more familiar and sure. We agreed on one other thing: We could not accept the limitations of our current situation.

What to do? We prayed, and prayed, and prayed some more, seeking God's guidance. Over the course of time, we held many meetings together, hoping that one or more of us would perceive a clear word from the Lord. We were getting nothing. Finally we were nearing the end of our "due diligence" period — we had to decide whether or not to buy the property.

We scheduled a congregational meeting, and right up to the moment we walked into the meeting, neither the lay leadership, nor I, had a clear understanding of which direction to go, despite our faith and trust that God would give at least one of us an answer to our prior persistent prayer. None of us knew which way we would vote; we offered a highly optimistic prayer that the congregation would reach consensus by the end of the meeting, even though the leadership had not been able to ascertain God's direction.

The meeting began in the usual way, with prayer and then a review of our journey up to that point, the information we had about the property, and the different possible scenarios of our financial situation if we bought the property. It was clear to me that, humanly speaking, buying the property was sheer insanity — financially speaking, there was no way these 100 generous-hearted people would be able to finance this venture. It was also clear to me, however, that God is not limited to that which is humanly possible, practical, or comfortable; therefore, common sense was not to be the measuring stick in this decision. I trusted that God's guidance would become clear in the meeting.

After several persons shared a variety of opinions and considerations, one of our members — usually quiet at meetings and very cautious regarding finances — walked up to the microphone, and began to list the names of former members who had passed on to glory, and their faithful activities and witness in the church. Many of these saints were relatives of those currently in the room. He concluded his talk by encouraging us to move forward with the purchase. From the minute he began to speak, it became apparent that we were receiving the word of the Lord for which we had so fervently prayed. The energy in the room became active and united, and from that moment on, there was only positive input as to what we should do. Consensus was obvious; we took a private paper vote to make sure, and all but one agreed that we were to go ahead with the purchase.

We all left the meeting in awe of what had happened — it was so obvious that the Spirit of God had filled that room, we haven't been the same since! We have grown tremendously — spiritually, and as a community — bonded to the mission of Christ. God has been so faithful — less than two years later, we are worshiping in our new church building, and now have visitors in worship every week. God is good.

I Will Not Forget You

J. Michael Mansfield

Can a woman forget her nursing child, or show no compassion for the child of her womb? Even these may forget, yet I will not forget you. See, I have inscribed you on the palms of my hands....
— Isaiah 49:15-16a

So do not worry about tomorrow, for tomorrow will bring worries of its own. Today's trouble is enough for today.   — Matthew 6:34

My best friend from seminary and his spouse were surprised and upset to learn that the third child they were expecting had Down's syndrome. They didn't have any warning. Some of their friends were adamant that, if they just prayed hard enough, this child, named "Joe," would be normal. They prayed. They tried to believe. Joe was born with Down's syndrome, and that was as "normal" as he would be.

We watched Joe grow up. We were present in their home when he had his first "solo" BM. We, along with his parents, were there to see the proud look on his face as he showed us his first poop. We were nearby when he developed respiratory infections, and ear infections, and finally hearing difficulties. Yes, Joe was a greater struggle than the other kids, but since his mom was a nurse, and both Mom and Dad were compassionate Christians, it didn't seem too difficult for them.

Four years after Joe's birth, my wife and I accompanied our friends to the Catholic Social Services building where we saw them receive their newly adopted child, Mike, who was also a Down's child. The miracle of healing had occurred. No, Joe's Down's wasn't eliminated. It was just that Down's syndrome had become something healthy in the vocabulary of his parents (and their friends as well). My friends had recognized that God had given them unique gifts for working with Down's syndrome children; and they wanted to share their gifts with another child with "the problem."

Joe graduated from high school and is now working full-time in the hospitality industry, in the laundry at a major hotel.

Mike is still in school. He will almost certainly graduate and go to work someday.

I often think of my friends and their four wonderful children, two of whom have greater challenges, when I hear of someone contemplating terminating a pregnancy. Most people, if given the time, would probably think that Joe and Mike were more blessing than difficulty. These two boys, now in their late teens and early twenties, are the most loving, huggable persons I have ever known.

Charlie Is Glowing

Deb Alexander

*And he was transfigured before them, and his face
shone like the sun, and his clothes became dazzling
white.* (v. 2)

On the evening of September 26, 2003, I received a telephone
call at about 10:15 p.m. from Allen, one of the partners in the
company where I am employed. This is a small, family owned
business, and having been there for thirteen years, I have been
treated as extended family. Allen informed me that his father, who
had been hospitalized for the past week, would probably not make
it through the night.

I immediately packed and drove the two hours, praying all the
way that God would keep Charlie with us long enough for me to
say good-bye. I have always carried guilt that I was not with my
own father when he passed. I arrived at the hospital in record time
and was able to sit with Charlie for about twenty minutes by myself, then off and on, as his family came and went. At about 4 a.m.
on Saturday, September 27, I went to my truck to get some medi-
cine I needed to take. As I walked across the parking lot, I prayed
to God to let Charlie pass quickly and peacefully, and, if it were
possible, to let Blanche, his wife who had passed before him, come
to take him home.

Charlie passed at 5:55 a.m. I remember standing with his sons
and their wives or girlfriends, each of us with a hand on Charlie so
he knew he wasn't alone. I remember trying to pray in my head,
and I was frustrated and angry because I couldn't remember words
that I had said so many times. Just after he passed, as his sons and
their partners wrapped their arms around one another in a group to
cry together, I stood at the foot of the bed. I thought one of the
girls came to stand beside me. Then I heard a voice say, "Look,

60

Charlie is glowing," and I looked. Charlie was surrounded by a beautiful, soft, white light, and his skin looked soft, white, and warm for a brief moment. Then the light went out. But as I looked around, no one else had moved from where they were, all wrapped in each other's arms, crying. I did not cry, and a peace came over me as I looked at what Charlie had left behind. I knew that it was Blanche's voice I had heard, that God had answered my prayer, and sent her to take Charlie home.

Lent

God does not die on the day when we cease to believe in a personal deity, but we die on the day when our lives cease to be illumined by the steady radiance, renewed daily, of a wonder, the source of which is beyond all reason.

Dag Hammarskjöld

Dag Hammarskjöld, *Markings* (New York: Knopf, 1964).

Still Learning Not To Wobble

Rosmarie Trapp

*Do not be like a horse or a mule, without under-
standing, whose temper must be curbed with a bit
and bridle, else it will not stay near you. Many
are the torments of the wicked, but steadfast love
surrounds those who trust in the Lord.* (vv. 9-10)

Some people accept the Lord Jesus Christ and live with that
for the rest of their lives. Others get inspired to proclaim him in
public for the rest of their lives. That's the way it is in our family,
and that's the way it is in the body of Christ, I think.

After I had said my Sinner's Prayer with an evangelist on the
radio in my bedroom one desperate night, I was having coffee in a
bus station and found a scripture on the wall. Put there by some
group for lost souls, it was Romans 10:9. It read:

*... If thou shalt confess with thy mouth the Lord Jesus,
and shalt believe in thine heart that God hath raised
him from the dead, thou shalt be saved.* (KJV)

That verse penetrated my terribly darkened mind, and my spirit
leaped up and said, "Yes, that's what I want!" But guess what? I
couldn't do it. There I sat, drinking coffee, and the word "Jesus"
would not come out of my mouth for my neighbor to hear. It was
stuck there, and I felt defeated again.

The Holy Spirit was trying to teach me what salvation is all
about. He led me gently, slowly, for I was a slow learner (and still
am!), but he never let me go. In my struggle to get back home and
start over again, these little penetrating lights got buried, and I
forgot them as being the important truths they are.

The mercy of God led me to the Community of the Crucified One. This group was in its beginning stages in Homestead, Pennsylvania. Eddie Donovan had been called by God to start a Bible study in his own house, and soon many people came, for he is an excellent Bible teacher.

One of the nuns from Baltimore told my sister, Agathe, about him, and as I had been living with her there for three years, we both flew to Homestead to have him talk with her. Soon my mother and other sisters came to hear him, and mother advised me to join his group. After another few years' struggle with rebellion, I submitted to the idea and drove to Homestead. It was May of 1978.

I was so warmly welcomed, and invited to stay as long as I felt I needed to. I decided to stay for two weeks. When I found out there was a trip to the Holy Land promised, I asked to go along. I was allowed to stay until October, and we had a glorious visit to the Holy Land.

As a result, Jesus came off the wall and out of pictures for me, and became a living person with history. That helped me decide to be part of the chapter of third order Franciscans.

There was much excitement when we returned to Homestead. I woke up every morning looking forward to what the day would bring. It was the beginning of our community, with many discussions and many decisions to be made. Everyone was included. Eddie was always talking in public and we were allowed to give our opinions. That was just up my alley, for I loved to be included in decision-making. When I was young, I had always envied my parents and siblings getting together to make decisions about the family singing group after Lorli and I, the little ones, had been put to bed.

Now I was part of another family — the family of God, making decisions. It was great! But one day I was disrespectful to authority. I forget what I said, but Eddie suggested a personal retreat might be helpful. It was my first extended retreat: It lasted seven days, and it got me to read the Bible. I found Paul talking to the women, telling them to be quiet in church in 1 Corinthians 14:34. That amazed me! Did Paul know I would be on a seven-day retreat because I had spoken out of turn? It made me quite self-conscious.

66

That evening, as I tried to fall asleep, the Lord visited me in a bright, golden light in my room. It made me remember the Sinner's Prayer I had said in Syracuse, New York. That was a real blessing. Praise God for his memory. He had not forgotten, even though I had. Through all the years I had spent in Baltimore, when people asked me how I had been saved, I couldn't say, because I had forgotten that simple prayer in my room. God is faithful, because he knew how distraught I had become about whether I was truly saved or not. He knew I would run up to the altar at every altar call, but it never reassured me. That night the golden glow brought peace to my soul, and I found that I could stand upon the rock of my salvation. At first I was pretty wobbly, and it took years to be firm. It's been twenty years since that blessing, and I'm still learning not to wobble.

Born Again

Kathy Raines

Jesus answered him, "Very truly I tell you, no one can see the kingdom of God without being born from above." (v. 3)

Larry lived across the street from the church in a low-income apartment complex. Several years before my husband and I came to the church as pastors, Larry had been in a very bad motorcycle accident. It wasn't certain that he would even live, but he did survive — with extensive brain damage. He learned to walk again, and most Sundays he would hobble across the street, with a bow-legged walk, to church. He'd climb the stairs and come into our adult Sunday school class, which met an hour before worship.

Many in the class were leaders of the church. Most of the owners of the town's Main Street businesses were active members. Some had been coming to the church for over fifty years. The Sunday school class members were literally doctors, lawyers, car dealers, and other prominent business men and women. Larry could not read and could barely write his name on the attendance pad. His sole subject of interest for conversation was motorcycles. I don't remember the topic at Sunday school that day, but we had veered into a discussion of worship. Then Larry blurted out, "I come to church because God saved my life."

Water Sign

Anne Sunday

> *Jesus said to her, "Everyone who drinks of this*
> *water will be thirsty again, but those who drink of*
> *the water that I will give them will never be thirsty.*
> *The water that I give will become in them a spring*
> *of water gushing up to eternal life.* (vv. 13-14)

The grotto below the little town of Emmittsburg, in the mountains of Maryland, was like an oasis to me in the midst of a dry and
barren time. It was a healing place for me every time I visited the
Lourdes Shrine and Resurrection Garden with the Stations of the
Cross. I went there to find refreshment and renewal, one hot summer day in the midst of a drought, at a time when my ministry
didn't seem to be very fruitful. I was on vacation, and the church I
was serving at that time was in the midst of conflict. As I thought
about the sad situation back at the church, I remembered the words
of the gospel writer, "... and he could do no good works there."

I also remembered how the Council President had looked at
me with wary eyes before I left, how he laughed nervously and
said, "Are you going to come back to us?" This gentle young man,
who was becoming more and more disgusted with the behavior of
some of his church family, knew he was reading my mind. A wise,
old seminary professor once said, "If you don't 'quit' the ministry
at least once a week, you're probably not doing your job!" Being
in the ministry is the most meaningful thing in my life, even if it is
often stressful.

And so, in the middle of my vacation, my friend Marilyn and
I eagerly headed onto the interstate that would take us across the
Pennsylvania line to the grotto. We wanted to find that special
spot again, in the woods above the healing pool of water at the

grotto, where we had spent a wonderful day, filled with peace, several years before.

Our plan was to hike up the mountain to look for the clearing we remembered, where we had spent an afternoon in silence — praying, meditating, and journaling — beside a bubbling brook. We found the clearing, but our joyful anticipation soon dissipated when we discovered that the streambed was completely dry. As I walked across it to the other side, looking around, I realized how much the drought had taken its toll. No wonder the healing pool had been roped off. A sign directed visitors to the pipe at the reservoir if they wanted to get a drink, fill bottles, or splash the water onto hands and faces. The stream came down from the mountain and fed into the pool, and now there was no water up there at all.

The dryness of the landscape matched the emptiness and loneliness in my soul. Spiritual dryness had taken its toll on me. Although disappointed, knowing we would miss the gentle sound of flowing water, we decided to make the best of it. God would still bless this day we had set aside for prayer. So, we trudged back down the mountain to retrieve our picnic lunch, Bibles, and journals from the car.

When we got back to the clearing we just stood there, dumbfounded. This wasn't possible! Now, the stream had water in it! We looked at each other with confusion and Marilyn said, "Are we going crazy? Wasn't this streambed completely dry a half hour ago?"

"Is it real?" I asked, thinking maybe it was a mirage.

I quickly dropped all my stuff on the ground, took off my sneakers and socks, and started wading around in the water, splashing it onto my arms and face. "No, it's real," I said. "It's really water. But, how did it get here?" Totally perplexed, I looked up to where the stream came down from a ledge above. The underbrush was so thick you couldn't see past where the water tumbled down over the ledge. It then gurgled over the rocks in the streambed, before disappearing into the woods at the other edge of the clearing.

"I can't believe it," we kept muttering over and over. "What does this mean?" Finally, we just gave up trying to explain it and settled down. We each staked out a spot in the clearing and turned our thoughts to God, enjoying several hours of solitary quiet time in peaceful prayer and reflection.

As we left the grounds of the grotto that day, and drove through the wrought iron gates to head back to the interstate, we couldn't stop talking about what had happened. "Do you think it was a miracle?" I asked.

"I don't know," Marilyn said.

"Well, do you think it would still be there if we turned around and went back up the mountain?"

"I don't know," she answered. "Maybe we should go find the Monsignor or someone and report that we've had a miracle!"

We weren't sure we wanted to tell anyone what had happened that day, lest they think we had both lost our minds, or worse yet, had made it all up. Some people I told just listened politely, giving me a blank look before changing the subject.

When I got back to the church after vacation, my friend Eileen called. She's a devout Catholic and a licensed therapist who was doing family counseling for our cluster of UCC churches. We would often get together at the end of a long day to have supper and discuss theology and life. When I told Eileen about the day at the grotto, she wasn't even surprised. "Of course it was real, Anne. God gave you a sign, in the midst of these difficult days, to encourage you, to let you know that he is with you."

The Gift Of Myself

Jim Eaton

... The Lord said, "Rise and anoint him; for this is the one." Then Samuel took the horn of oil, and anointed him in the presence of his brothers; and the spirit of the Lord came mightily upon David from that day forward. (vv. 12b-13a)

We know how changed we are when someone embraces the child within us. In 1965, I was a fourteen-year-old geek in the ninth grade at Bloomfield Junior High School on Quarton Road. My family had moved to Michigan a couple of years before and I'd been sick for a year, so I hadn't really found a place or a circle of friends. My English teacher was Mrs. Sonneborne, a towering cyclone of energy five feet tall, who invariably wore spiky high heels. Her room was arranged with the desks in a circle and she would walk around and around as she read to us from Shakespeare. This was during Beatlemania and the boys had been growing out their hair since seventh grade; and the girls all had long hair, too. Mrs. Sonneborne insisted on being able to look people in the eye, and when your bangs were too long, she would pick up a hair clip as she went by her desk, and on her next circuit she would deftly pin up the offending hair. Being "pinned" once was more than enough to get her point.

One day, Mrs. Sonneborne assigned everyone to rewrite a folk tale. I'd been reading a lot of drama, so I decided to write a play. It was five pages long, typed in dialogue format, and when I showed it to Mrs. Sonneborne, she had two other kids in the class act it out. It was — and is! — a heady feeling to watch someone speak lines you've written. After class, Mrs. Sonneborne kept me for a moment and said something I've never forgotten. "Jim, I didn't know what you were until today. Now I know; you're a writer."

And I was. I was still a geek, but I wasn't just a geek, I was a writer. I wrote two more plays for Mrs. Sonneborne, and others after that. A few years later, it occurred to me that writing a worship service was a lot like writing plays, and here I am, still at it. Mrs. Sonneborne was right: I'm a writer, and she saw it. She gave it to me. She surprised me with the gift of myself.

The Wandering Eye

Paul Calkin

To set the mind on the flesh is death, but to set the mind on the Spirit is life and peace ... But you are not in the flesh; you are in the Spirit, since the Spirit of God dwells in you. Anyone who does not have the Spirit of Christ does not belong to him. (vv. 6, 9)

I remember a teacher. We first called her Mrs. Lofton. She taught us Sunday school in the basement of the church. She used these flannelgraphs: They were flannel boards that she placed objects on, and moved them around, to teach us Bible stories. I was in the third grade at the time. We had a large class, probably twenty kids, so she had the corner of the basement because it had the most room. She always had a beautiful smile and a wonderful hug for everyone. One morning, she seemed a bit sad, however, and one of my classmates said to her just a few minutes into the lesson, "Mrs. Lofton, my mom said we should pray for you today."

So we gathered in a circle as Mrs. Lofton had taught us to do, and we held hands, and we prayed for her. Tears streamed down her face, and because she cried, we cried. We didn't find out until a few minutes later why we prayed for her. Her husband, Woody, had died Saturday afternoon. Yet Mrs. Lofton came to be with us that Sunday morning. Her children, and most of her family, attended that church. She got her best care there. That morning she needed to be there.

Over the next few months, we noticed a change in Mrs. Lofton. She was sad. The smile was gone. The hugs weren't as frequent. We wanted to help, but we just didn't know what to do. We decided, as a class, that we would pray for her, and so we did. After a few months, her spirits began to brighten a bit, and we thought that it was our prayers. We felt pretty good about that. Time went by.

Then, one day, an announcement was made in church that she was getting married. I heard the gentleman sitting beside me say it was "too soon ... wasn't a proper length of time." I didn't know what that meant. All I knew was that I wanted her to be happy.

After worship, some of us children overheard the adults say something about the man that she was going to marry. They said that he had a "wandering eye." When we met him, we decided that the left one did float a bit to the left. Why that could possibly worry someone, we didn't know. We just knew that she seemed happy.

They had been married about a year. Suddenly, one Sunday morning, her new husband, Leonard, walked down the aisle of the church, made his profession of faith, and was baptized. Those of us who had been in her Sunday school class stood up in the back of the church and cheered.

They say his eye never wandered again. I still think it drifted to the left. Leonard became one of the best workers in that church, and one of the most committed Christians that I have ever met.

Holy Week
And Easter

At heart, religion is mysticism. Moses with his
flocks in Midian, Buddha under the Bo tree, Jesus
up to his knees in the waters of the Jordan: each
of them responds to Something for which words
like shalom, oneness, God even, are only pallid
souvenirs. "I have seen things," Acquinas told a
friend, "that make all my writings feel like straw."

Frederick Buechner

Having visions does not mean that I am less fal-
lible than others. No matter how vivid spiritual
experiences become, they are not direct sightings
of God. "We see in a mirror dimly," as Saint Paul
wrote. Pop, my Cherokee grandfather, put it this
way: "The angel tells it right, but none of us hear
angels all that good."

Eddie Ensley

Frederick Buechner, *A Room Called Remember: Uncollected
Pieces* (New York: Harper and Row, 1992), pp. 151.

Eddie Ensley, *Visions: The Soul's Path To The Sacred* (Chi-
cago: Loyola Press, 2000), p. 32.

Forsaken?

Judith B. Brain

My God, my God, why have you forsaken me? Why
are you so far from helping me, from the words of
my groaning?   — Psalm 22:1

I got a panicky phone call from a parishioner. "Kate" was going through a terrible time. Her daughter had been hospitalized after attempting suicide, another manifestation of severe psychological trauma resulting from a childhood rape.

In addition, Kate was in the middle of divorcing her emotionally-abusive husband and her son was acting out because of all the turmoil in their lives. Now, her job was threatened because she'd had to take too much time off to care for her daughter and shepherd her son through his troubles.

She was distraught when she asked me to come over. Thinking about all the stresses in her life made me wonder how I would be an effective pastor in this overwhelmingly difficult situation. On the drive to her house, I reviewed all of the things I'd learned in counseling and pastoral care courses. "Let her express her fears and anger. Stay with the pain. Don't try to solve anything. Respect her feelings of loss and abandonment...."

When I got to the house she pulled me inside, and before I said a word, she looked me straight in the eye and said, "I don't need you to sit here and listen to my pain and give me an opportunity to express my feelings. I've got a shrink for that. I want *you* to tell me why God is doing this to me!"

Easter Stories

... but God raised him on the third day and allowed him to appear, not to all the people but to us who were chosen by God as witnesses, and who ate and drank with him after he rose from the dead. (vv. 40-41)

Ralph Milton

Not long ago, at about 9:00 on a Sunday night, I had a call from my sister, Peggy, saying that our sister, June, had died. It was not an unexpected death. June was cursed with a tobacco addiction she was never able to shake, and so the last years of her life were spent in a half-life of emphysema, hooked up to oxygen, struggling to breathe. June was a vivacious, joyous, musical person, and it caused us much pain to see her living that way. Her death, when it came, was a blessing.

But, I grieved anyway. That night, as I went to bed, I suddenly found myself with June and Peggy, and we were singing together as we often did as children — loud and high and clear in our childhood voices, the songs from Humperdink's *Hansel and Gretel*: "When at night I go to sleep, fourteen angels watch do keep ..." and the final line, "two to whom 'tis given to guide my steps to heaven."

This was not just a memory. It was far too clear and powerful, and I sang through the whole song, every word, with my sisters. I don't know if I was asleep or not. I don't think I was. I don't recall ever having a memory or a dream as clear and powerful as that one. It left me with a sense of joy and peace and thanksgiving.

I've told a number of people about that vision, and in each telling, and the feedback that it brings, I've understood it a bit more, and valued it more deeply, as my farewell to a much-treasured sister.

Lisa Lancaster

John and I were good friends. His wife, Katie, and I just remained acquaintances. Then I found out that Katie had cancer, and that it had progressed to the point that there was no hope for recovery. I was able to be a support to John, but Katie pushed me away, right up until the very end. I always felt so unsettled that I had been able to help him, but not her, or their three children. I had this nagging feeling for weeks that I had not done enough.

Then, one night, I dreamed about Katie. She walked toward me, with her hand outstretched for a handshake, and said to me, "I want to thank you for all that you did for my family." I knew it was actually a visitation, and I have always been grateful to God for this, and to Katie, for reassuring me in a way that finally enabled me to let go.

Ned Dorau

I recently baptized the second daughter of an Arizona couple, Kris and Mark. They had journeyed to Random Lake, Wisconsin, with the baby and their first daughter, Alexandra. Kris is originally from a Catholic family in the area, and her husband Mark, a Lutheran, is from Eau Claire. They are both active members of a Lutheran church in Arizona, and they thought that by having the baptism here, the whole family could be present for the joy that is always part of that special day. Many from the Catholic side of the family came to church that Sunday in late November, and we celebrated together during the liturgy and afterwards. I had the privilege of meeting Kris's dad, Tom, who, with his wife, had been a lifelong Random Lake resident before moving to Plymouth the previous year, for health reasons.

Several days later, Kris sent me an e-mail with a wonderful picture from the baptism, and the sad news that her dad, Tom, whom I had met less than two weeks earlier, had suffered a massive stroke and had irreversible brain damage.

The funeral was yesterday, and I once again connected with the whole family, this time at the Catholic church. As I greeted Tom's wife and daughter, Kris, they shared a special story about Alexandra. A couple of days before her mother called Kris in Arizona to tell her of her dad's death, Kris had noticed her little daughter Alexandra returning again and again to a wedding picture she had in the kitchen of her with her parents. Each time Alexandra came to the picture she would say, "Mommy, Grandma, Grandpa. Grandpa go bye-bye." The statement concerned Kris so much that she immediately called her parents to make sure her father was all right. She was relieved when her father answered the phone. He talked to her about what a beautiful day it was and how much he was enjoying it.

A couple of days later, the call came from Wisconsin, confirming what little Alexandra had already sensed. The family understands her experience as a special moment for them, reinforcing the belief that the Lord indeed works in mysterious and wonderful ways.

Hoo

Claire Clyburn

When it was evening on that day, the first day of the week, and the doors of the house where the disciples had met were locked for fear of the Jews, Jesus came and stood among them and said, "Peace be with you." After he said this, he showed them his hands and his side. Then the disciples rejoiced when they saw the Lord. (vv. 19-20)

I went to visit my parents one Sunday afternoon, following our Easter worship service. They had a collection of old college yearbooks on the kitchen table and I sat down to have a look. They were from the 1920s and were yearbooks from my grandparents' college years. I recognized my grandmother's picture in *The Oak Leaves*, Meredith College's annual. I tried to imagine her as a young woman, nineteen years old, with a flapper haircut and stylish dresses. Her smile was demure, even as a young woman. For the first time, I could see a little bit of my mother in her.

I found my grandfather's yearbooks — *The Howler* from Wake Forest University. It only took a minute to find his portrait, class of 1926. I couldn't believe my eyes — here was a handsome young man with a half-smile, round Harry Potter glasses, light brown hair, fit and trim, with his whole life ahead of him. There was an air of expectancy about him. I put those two pictures side by side, my grandfather's and my grandmother's, and wondered what had drawn them together a few years later when they were both teaching at the Morehead School for the Blind.

When my grandfather was in his sixties, he retired from teaching at UNC-Wilmington and spent the rest of his days on the sound. He made and mended nets during the day, fished in the early morning hours, according to the tide, built houses or did other carpentry work as time allowed. Every afternoon he took a nap on the swing couch on his front porch. Though there was no air conditioning in the house, the constant breezes coming from the water had a natural cooling effect, and Granddaddy fell asleep curled up on his side with a gentle breeze wafting over him. When I think of him now, that is how I usually picture him — curled up in a fetal position on that couch, like a tiger taking his noonday rest. As we grew, he took pride in teaching us the old ways, and he wanted to see our muscles, especially after spending a day working with him in the shop, or on the boat. My brothers would make a fist with pride, and my cousin, Laura, and I also would flex our biceps, not knowing that it wasn't ladylike. He would feel our growing muscles and we would beg him to do the same. At sixty and seventy years of age, he would flex his bicep and a muscle the size and hardness of a major league baseball would pop up without difficulty.

He lived to be 89, and worked every day but Sunday all of his life. He neither smoked nor drank alcohol, ate the freshest foods he could find, what he caught from the sound and what he got from the garden; he drank mostly water, huge glasses on the table at every meal, and a cup of coffee in the morning. He loved coconut cake, but otherwise ate few sweets, even on holidays.

Grandma taught first grade for over thirty years before she retired. Once she retired, her time was taken up caring for a granddaughter who lived nearby. I never saw her walk anywhere; she scurried and hurried like a mouse from the stove to the sink to the porch to the laundry to the bathroom to the living room. When she needed Granddaddy she went to the front door and yelled, "Adrian!" "Hoo!" he would call back. She worked sunup 'til sundown as well and couldn't stand the idea that you might do something for her, so that she could sit down and rest. He went to bed no later than 9 p.m., no matter where he was. She stayed up to read, her one passion.

I remember one of the last times I saw them before Granddaddy's failing health landed him in the hospital for the last three days of his long life. It was over New Year's, near his birthday, and my brother and I went to see them for the day. We brought a meal with us so that neither of them would feel obliged to cook. The year before we had taken a Christmas tree to decorate so that Grandmama would have one in her home. I have a photo of the two of them, married over fifty years, sitting on their couch, and the couch nearly swallowing them whole. I remember distinctly how long it took them to stand up from a sitting position, how many times he would start up with his arms, like they were propellers giving him extra momentum, until he could halfway stand in a bent-over position. Two or three more pumps with his arms and he would be upright, his breath punctuated with snorts and grunts as his legs limbered up and he tried to walk.

I put these images together — this twenty-year-old young man in fighting trim, the sixty-year-old man whose bicep would have given Arnold Schwarzenegger a fright, and this 89-year-old man whose body was beginning to fail him. Old age, says my dad, isn't for sissies.

He was lying on his side in a fetal position when I saw him last. If it weren't for the fact that we were in a hospital, it could have been another sunny day on the front porch, him taking a nap under the shade and breeze. He was in pain as his kidneys began to shut down and didn't have much energy for words. "I love you, Granddaddy." "Hoo."

Seeing him dead, that bicep no longer flexed, those bright studious eyes forever closed, the half-smile drawn and mercilessly still, I gave thanks for my Christian faith, which teaches me to believe in a resurrection of the body.

I often wonder how I will recognize my grandfather when I see him again. Will it be by his bicep? His half-smile? Will he be curled up on a couch where the breeze comes off the sound? Will I call him and hear him answer, "Hoo!"?

Stranger In The Choir

Martha Hartman

When he was at the table with them, he took bread,
blessed and broke it, and gave it to them. Then
their eyes were opened and they recognized him;
and he vanished from their sight. They said to each
other, "Were not our hearts burning within us
while he was talking to us on the road, while he
was opening the scriptures to us?" (vv. 30-32)

One Sunday, as I was walking from the parsonage to the church, I noticed a stranger crouched between two bushes, against the wall of the church, near the front entrance. My heart skipped a beat. Could it be? But, before I could pursue that thought further, my attention was diverted by three "regulars" getting out of a car and chatting with one another. One called, "Good morning, Pastor." I waved and shouted a good morning in return.

I looked back at the stranger. She was middle-aged, dressed in a colorful, very thin broomstick skirt, a loose-fitting and wrinkled cotton top, sandals with no stockings of any sort, and a wide-brimmed, floppy black and white checkered hat. She was hurriedly putting out a cigarette in the dirt near one of the bushes. I approached her and gave a cheerful, "Hi!" She said, "Hi," in return.

Her bangs were long and straight, and fell down over her eyes. She wore no make-up, and her face, slightly scarred and slightly puffy, made me think she'd been places and seen things that most of us could not imagine — or could *only* imagine. "How are you today?" I asked.

"Fine," she replied, "how are you?"

"I'm fine, too." I said. The three regulars were coming up the sidewalk behind me, and trusting them, knowing them well enough

86

to know they would also greet her, I decided to keep moving and let them talk to her.

Inside the church, I had the normal Sunday morning encounters with a half-dozen or so people as I made my way to my office to put on my robe. Once robed, I ran down the stairs to say a prayer with the choir, and, lo and behold, the stranger was standing with them! As I approached the group, one of the choir members asked the stranger if she'd like to join them — to robe up and sit with them in the choir loft. She said she would like that, and a minute or two later, there she stood, dressed in a choir robe, holding a songbook, and singing her heart out with the others; the wide-brimmed, floppy black and white checkered hat still on her head, her long, straight bangs still covering her eyes.

One of the older choir members said, with just the right touch of frankness and love, "We don't need the hat." The stranger removed the hat. Her layered, straight hair, filled with static electricity, went every which way — mostly up! She tried to smooth it down.

I asked her name, so I could introduce her during our time for announcements. She told me, and added that her maiden name was such and such. A choir member said, "Oh! Are you related to the 'so and so's' who were members here?" Yes, she was; they were her parents, now deceased.

"Oh, I remember you!" another choir member exclaimed.

"And I remember your parents," someone else said. "They gave us our communion set!"

Our communion set ... think of the symbolism in that! Our stranger had come home, and, thanks be to God, her family-in-Christ had not ignored her, nor cast fearful glances at her, but had welcomed her into the very center of our choir-fold.

Holy Hands

David Michael Smith

The Lord is my shepherd, I shall not want. He
makes me lie down in green pastures; he leads me
beside still waters; he restores my soul. He leads
me in right paths for his name's sake. (vv. 1-3)

Five years shy of a century, my grandfather, Oscar Bailey, felt
old. Ironically, you would think that would be natural, but then
again, you'd have to personally know Oscar. Old age and the man
never meshed. It was as if he had discovered the fountain of youth,
if not physically, then mentally, and would live forever.

Each summer he would plant a picturesque, weedless garden,
comparable to the ones you'd see in the pages of *Southern Living,*
each row perfectly straight, each cultivated plant colorful and leafy.
He'd use a plumb line to insure accuracy, and plowed with a thirty-
year-old rototiller, daily.

Well into his nineties you'd find him motoring all over the
county in his Chevy, sharpening chainsaw blades, stacking wood,
cleaning his chimney, visiting the barber, and mowing his own
grass, often opting to use the push mower over the rider. He behaved like a man half his age, even younger, and always lived life
to its fullest. But then, seemingly all at once, old age breathlessly
caught him on the racetrack of life. With achy limbs and a bad
back, plus a hazardous heart condition, he felt exhausted, depressed.

The plummet began two years prior when his beloved wife,
my grandmother, Mildred, six years younger than her partner of
seventy years, fell ill. On a cold winter's day in January, during a
routine stop at the convenience store for a jug of milk, she collapsed without warning in the parking lot. She spent weeks in the
hospital recuperating, but never fully recovered. Doctors could
not pinpoint the root cause for the fall, but it was speculated she

had suffered a minor stroke. At the same time, the stubborn symptoms of Alzheimer's began to manifest, along with other physical and mental infirmities. Mildred was sick, and she'd never be the way she was before.

For decades, the couple had lived happy, blessed lives, partly because they rose early, worked hard, ate well, avoided television, embraced honesty, defended America, made no enemies, and slept well. They were children of European immigrants, and the types of people who loved their country during both the rich and frail times.

Oscar had been a forester, now long retired, and could tell you every variety of plant and tree in the woods. He once hunted and fished alone from an old, wooden rowboat, but it had been years since he last cast his line. He made his own wine, from blackberries, blueberries, and purple grapes, and smoked a pipe for many years in the comforts of his old tin-roofed work shed.

For many years Mildred cooked every meal from scratch, often using the vegetables and fruits grown from their annual garden. She canned jams, relishes, and tomatoes. Every baked cake was homemade, and the icing, buttery rich in flavor.

The house was always spotless, the floors waxed and shiny. She was an avid duster, and swept the kitchen and porch floors at least three times a day, sometimes more. But those days were behind the elderly couple, now distant memories.

The same woman who once lived the life of *Good Housekeeping*'s centerfold now spent most of her hours in bed with the covers pulled to her chin, sleeping in a dark, dreary room, even while the sun shone outside. Oscar woke her up to eat and take medication, but she seemed most comfortable alone and tucked away in solitude of her bedroom.

Oscar, for years the breadwinner, now became the jack and queen of all trades. Chores and duties long held by his wife became his responsibilities by default. He did the laundry, prepared the meals, handled the bills, and washed the dishes. But when you're 95, handling daily chores ardently takes a toll on your body and soul, especially with a woman around who doesn't always recognize you and is unpredictable in her behavior.

The couple received help from relatives, chiefly their daughter, Phyllis, who visited daily, bringing groceries and words of good cheer. Family members helped with running errands and doing yard work, but Oscar and Mildred were proud people, and came from a generation where help, even from loving family members, was considered a handout. That was generally unacceptable to a man and woman who initially refused to accept Social Security when they reached retirement age, since to them, that was money they had not worked to earn.

The subject of a retirement home was raised on occasion, but Oscar would have no part of the conversation.

"We have been in this house for years," he proudly proclaimed, "and we'll die in this house, not a 'home.' " He meant every word of it and despite the pitfalls of an elderly couple struggling with their aches and pains and ailments, the family honored their wishes.

Each day was a struggle, and one day things came to a head. Oscar was exhausted from a day of dealing with a woman whom he dearly loved, but was at the same time no longer that same woman he cared so deeply for. Working around the home had worn him out, and his body simply ached to the core. He felt like he'd run a marathon, and could barely move. Specifically, his back hurt beyond description, from his tailbone to his neck, every vertebrae throbbing with irritation and fatigue. How could he go on like this? He couldn't.

He collapsed against an ancient sofa in the shadowy living room as night cast a cloak upon the earth outside. Sitting there in a pool of pain and depression he reached around to rub his lower back, utterly spent of energy. Hot tears welled up in his eyes. He wondered with frustration from where his strength to survive would come, and he moaned a desperate prayer. He simply could not abandon his bride, the only woman he ever loved or could love. Then he felt two hands.

"Mildred, what on earth are you doing, woman?" he asked incredulously, surprised his wife had come out of her room at this late hour.

He turned around to face his wife, but she was not there. To his surprise, *no one* was there! Yet the presence of two hands upon his back remained, invisible, massaging hands, which clasped his with gentleness and love.

Oscar did not move, but not out of fear. He calmly faced the unseen visitor, then stared at his hands, but could see nothing. Sure, his eyesight wasn't what it had once been, but with his glasses, he could see very well. No one was with him. The room was empty of humankind. It was empty of any visible spirit form. But he felt the hands, the fingers and palms, of a man.

The presence massaged his hands in a merciful manner, slowly, and with care. Warm waves rushed through Oscar, radiating across his decrepit body, and he was comforted. For a few moments, the supernatural event continued, and the pains of his body and spirit were replaced by a deep, serene peace. It was at that moment he knew he was in the presence of his Lord, the Savior, who died for him two millenniums ago.

Jesus departed, and soon the aches and pains returned. But, Oscar knew he had been visited by God, and from the wordless exchange between earthly and holy hands, he knew that things were going to be all right.

A Rock Of Refuge

Jody E. Felton

Incline your ear to me; rescue me speedily. Be a rock of refuge for me, a strong fortress to save me. You are indeed my rock and my fortress; for your name's sake lead me and guide me, take me out of the net that is hidden for me, for you are my refuge. Into your hand I commit my spirit; you have redeemed me, O Lord, faithful God. (vv. 2-5)

On July 10, 2000, a great man died. The world may not have known a great man died, but his wife knew, his children and his grandchildren knew, and the people who crowded into the church for the memorial service knew. That great man was my father.

Dad died in 2000, but we began losing him to Alzheimer's Disease about ten years before. Medication slowed the process, but it was still a tragedy that we had to deal with daily ... sometimes with anger, sometimes with tears, sometimes with acceptance, and as often as possible, with a sense of humor.

My father, himself, helped us accept his condition. He had been diagnosed at a time when he was still able to understand what it meant to have Alzheimer's. He accepted the diagnosis with his usual grace and good humor. Years before, he had started losing his hearing. He was totally deaf without his hearing aids, but he accepted deafness as a fact of life. For him, Alzheimer's was just another fact of life to be accepted.

Actually, for Dad, Alzheimer's wasn't so bad. He had moments when he got frustrated, especially in the early stages, when the confusion got too bad, or when he struggled to find the right word. However, Dad was one of those people who was unflappable, and those times did not last too long. For Dad, every day was new and every experience was new. He hadn't seen a rerun in years ... every program was new, no matter how many times he had seen it. He, unlike the rest of us, never ate leftovers. Every meal was a new meal.

It was harder for us to cope with his Alzheimer's. My dad, as I remember him, almost totally disappeared by six or seven years into the disease. He used to get up every morning and say something like, "Do you know what happened thirteen years ago today?" Of course, we never did. But Dad knew. It was always something that had stayed in his mind, long after the rest of us had forgotten it ... some bit of trivia like, "That was the day we bought that old El Camino" or "That was the day the Holstein cow had twins." As the disease progressed he couldn't remember thirteen minutes ago, much less thirteen years ago.

Dad used to tell wonderful stories about his life. Then the stories got more and more confused. He had trouble forming complete sentences, and words often escaped him. Eventually he gave up talking all together.

Despite all that, when we gather around the Thanksgiving table this Thursday, I will be giving thanks for my father ... not just for who he was before Alzheimer's, but for who he became, and for the lessons I learned from him as he coped with the disease. For you see, even though I do not believe God causes tragedy so we can learn lessons and grow, I do believe that God intervenes in every tragedy. If we pay attention, we learn and we grow stronger. Let me share with you what I have to be thankful for from my dad's Alzheimer's, and what I learned about God from it.

Probably, the hardest thing to cope with was when Dad began losing people. The first to go was my youngest brother, John. At the time, John and his family lived in Ohio. Mom and Dad lived in Pasco, Washington. They rarely saw John ... only once or twice a year. Dad forgot that John was his son. He thought John was Mom's son, which is true, but for a while Dad thought Mom was his second wife. Nobody knows why. Despite all that, Dad had a great fondness for John.

During that time, my sister and her family lived with Mom and Dad while they made arrangements to buy the house, so Mom and Dad could move to a retirement center. Almost daily, after

John had been there for a visit, Dad would ask Merrie if she knew John. She would always reply, "Yes," she knew John. Dad always responded, "I really like John. He is such a nice guy. A peach of a guy. (Dad's highest praise for anyone.) He is so nice. He just likes to be nice."

Over the years, Dad lost all five of us. He was always delighted to see us, but he did not know we were his children. Dad was the epitome of "forgetful love." He loved John and the rest of us even though he did not know we were his children. Dad forgot all the times we were disrespectful, the times we disappointed him, the times we neglected to be grateful for all he was to us. He just remembered that he loved us. He forgot the less than wonderful in us, but remembered the love.

One of the surprises for me was what my father did remember. My daughter, Katy, got married nine years ago in July. Katy was Dad's oldest grandchild. Dad went to the wedding, the proudest grandpa you've ever seen. The wedding was in Salem, Oregon. When we were going back to Pasco the next day, Dad kept asking me why we were going east. I told him we were going to his house in Pasco. His reply was, "Do I live in Pasco? How long have I lived there?" The answer was, "over thirty years."

Dad did not remember where he lived, but he could, and did, recall small details of the wedding. Over the years after the wedding, when he had forgotten most everything else, he would talk about "the one who got married."

Katy and Brian now have six-year-old twin daughters ... my granddaughters, Dad's great-granddaughters. Dad never knew they were his great-granddaughters, but he always delighted in them and he always remembered them when they visited him. It was as if there was something too important about weddings and babies for Dad to forget.

After more than fifty years of marriage, despite the Alzheimer's, Dad still dearly loved Mom. There came a time when Dad forgot he was married. He would ask Mom, "Do I have a wife?" She answered, "Yes." Then he asked, "Who is my wife?" When she replied that she was his wife, Dad would smile and his whole face beamed with joy. Then he would say, "I'm glad you are my wife." For a while, Dad asked Mom to marry him at least twice a day ... just in case she wasn't already his wife.

With Mom, Dad forgot himself, in his love for her. He was always reaching out to enfold her in love. Some instinctive part of him knew that love needs to be shared. He wanted to share it with the one who had shared his love for over fifty years, proving that love is stronger than all else, even Alzheimer's.

Once when I was visiting Dad, as I got ready to go home, Dad wanted to give me something. He reached into his pocket and pulled out a little, round rock. Then he said to me, "I keep this in my pocket so when I get confused and upset, I just rub it until I feel better. I want you to have it."

That rock is my most prized possession. I keep it with me always. Dad told me he loved me in the only way he could. By giving me something precious to him, he was really giving me a piece of himself.

I Will Not Leave You Orphaned

Lori Hetzel

I will not leave you orphaned; I am coming to you.
In a little while the world will no longer see me,
but you will see me; because I live, you also will
live. On that day you will know that I am in my
Father, and you in me, and I in you.
                                    — John 14:18-20

But truly God has listened; he has given heed to
the words of my prayer.   — Psalm 66:19

A year ago, my husband and I traveled to the country of
Kazahstan to adopt our daughter, Delaney. We left our two boys at
home with my husband's parents who came up from Tucson to
stay with them. Our estimated time to be away from the United
States was five weeks. We had to travel to Frankfurt, Germany,
then on to Kostanai, Kazahstan. My husband, Karl, was very anx-
ious about the language barrier. While on the plane to Germany,
he prayed over and over again that we would meet someone who
spoke English to help us go through customs. While we waited in
Germany to board the plane to Kazahstan, a young man spoke to
us ... yes, in English! He was a Peace Corps volunteer traveling
back to Kazahstan. Relief swept over my husband, and he con-
fided in this man about his prayer being answered. He helped us
get through customs and retrieve our luggage. I told Karl that this
man was an angel brought here to help us on our journey.

We visited the orphanage on the first day with our translator,
Eugene. Before entering the orphanage, you must first open a big
door. Inside there was a lace curtain that you must pull aside. The
moment I touched that curtain an overwhelming feeling of déjà vu
passed through me. I had dreamed of this place before we traveled

there. The only thing missing was women dressed in white coats greeting us as we came in. I saw the dark, narrow hallway, and expected the women to appear. It was powerful. Our translator told us that he had a strong sense of déjà vu the moment he saw us. "It was as if I had known you all my life."

We met our daughter, who had been abandoned by her mother at just over two months and left to die under a stairwell. A police officer found her and took her to the hospital, where they cared for her, and named her Diana. We renamed her Delaney Diana. Things were going fine until we moved on to another part of Kazahstan. We had a bit of trouble with our new daughter's visa. The official who was to sign it had left for another area of the country, so our associate told us we might as well go on to Almaty, to meet with the consular there until Delaney's visa came through.

Back at home, our youngest son, Connor, was very ill with croup and bronchitis, and nearly had to be hospitalized. We were terribly homesick and my husband was battling with panic attacks and stomach upset. We spent hours praying that we would meet someone in Almaty who spoke English. We were only supposed to spend two days in the hotel, which cost about $300 a day. We ended up staying for five days and were rapidly running out of money. We did not know when the official would return to sign the visa so we could move on to Moscow to get Delaney's entry visa to the U.S. We prayed for a new translator.

We met this new translator (answered prayer) in the lobby of our hotel. Both Karl and I were having a hard time holding it all together. All we wanted was to go home. As we sat in the lobby, a woman stopped at our table, asked if we were American, and if we had adopted our daughter. Now, we had been warned not to discuss why we were there with anyone, so I lied and told the woman no. When she walked away, I felt horrible for lying to her, but I believed it was for our safety. I watched as she sat down nearby. Then I left our table, sat down next to her, and I cried. I was having a nervous breakdown in front of a total stranger in a strange country. She calmed me down with her sweet voice and compassionate eyes. An angel? I asked myself silently. She told me she seldom came to the hotel to get work done, but today it seemed like a good idea. Her family was originally from Colorado, and they were missionaries there in Kazahstan. She prayed for us, and told me that she had three biological sons and had adopted a daughter there, also.

She invited us for dinner at her house. She told us she would be busy the next day, but to call her if we needed anything, then we all held hands and prayed.

Time passed and we still didn't have Delaney's visa. Staying in the hotel was costing us more than we had planned. Karl paced the floor everyday, praying. We needed a new place to stay, and if the visa did not arrive by Friday, I would have to go to Moscow alone and leave Delaney somewhere, so Karl could go back to work.

We called upon our "angel." She took us into her home for five days, fed us, and let us have her home as if it was ours. She spoke fluent Russian, so she could help us with the visa arrangements. Finally, the visa came and we were able to go on to Moscow.

If it wasn't for this woman appearing, by the grace of God, we would have been lost. We will never forget the work of our gracious Lord, who sends those earthly angels to help those in need.

Lambasting God

Maria Seifert

Humble yourselves therefore under the mighty
hand of God, so that he may exalt you in time.
Cast all your anxieties on him because he cares
for you.   — 1 Peter 5:6-7

My mother, Eva, was born in the back woods of south Texas in 1934. Her family was very poor and she was the third child of ten. When Mom was a little girl, she contracted strep throat and, due to the poverty of the Great Depression, it was left untreated. As a result, Mom suffered significant heart damage and heart problems plagued her all of her life.

At the young age of 65, Mom suffered a stroke, which drastically changed her personality. She went from watching Milwaukee Public Television and Christian preachers to never missing an episode of Jerry Springer. Mom would actually shush us if we dared to talk before a commercial! She became self-centered, selfish, impatient, full of self-pity and anger, and physically violent. Thankfully, my father had quick reflexes, so there was never any real damage done. Simply put, Mom changed to the opposite of the mom that I had known so well and loved so much. This didn't dampen my love for her, and I continued to support and nurture this new person who became so uncharacteristically dependent on anyone within arm's reach.

One morning, Mom's blood pressure became dangerously high, resulting in a hospital stay and a battery of tests. On the evening she was supposed to return home, the doctor requested that she stay just one more night for an additional test that couldn't be administered until the next morning. Mom suffered multiple strokes in her sleep that night and never regained consciousness.

When there was nothing more the hospital could do for her, Mom was moved to a nursing home. I scheduled meetings with the admissions staff to get information and paperwork. I was informed that, when my father could no longer afford to pay for Mom's care privately, she would become a Medicaid patient. In order to qualify for Medicaid, pretty much everything but the spouse's home and vehicle would have to be liquidated. My mom was a teacher for 39 years and my father was a longshoreman. They spent years saving their money to live their retirement years comfortably, with a home in the city, and their small cottage up north. All of their saving and the fruits of their labor would be for naught. I had to explain this to my father several times, in two languages. I knew it finally registered when I saw insecurity in his eyes during one conversation. I had never seen that look in my father before.

I was so angry that night, it was radiating from my body. No one in the family even dared talk to me. I was blaming no one but God for the whole mess, and I let him have it when I prayed, if you could even call it praying. I started ranting at about 9 p.m. and the last time I looked at the clock it was about 1 a.m. I lambasted God for not taking my mom to heaven. She had spent her entire life listening to, reading, and living his word, teaching it to children and adults alike. She was humble, generous, selfless, obedient, and above all, she made people happy. Why was she not in heaven? If this was part of his plan, I needed God to know that I thought it really sucked! I also told him that, up until that day, I was one of his biggest fans. This is actually quite a mild interpretation of my one-way conversation with God that night.

I awoke the next morning with a very heavy heart. My eyes were puffy from crying and my chest hurt from too much raw emotion. The first thought that entered my mind as I sat up in bed was, "Your dad is not ready to let her go yet. Until he is ready, she will stay." I received that message, the first of many that day, from a little voice inside my head that just so happened to speak in the third person. I wondered if it was my ever-present guardian angel passing on a message, since I was sure God didn't want anything to do with me after the previous night. Or may be it *was* God! I prayed silently and sheepishly, "I'm so very sorry for everything I said last night ... and early this morning ... for every mean thought I had of you. I take it all back. I don't even feel worthy to receive your message. Thank you for that. Thank you for finding me worthy and for forgiving and loving me. I am sorry I slandered your plan."

I went to work that morning mostly for the distraction. Then the little voice said, "Leave right now and pick up your sister. Get to the nursing home immediately." I went at once. My sister, her children, my father, Tia Emma and Uncle Frank, and I were sitting in my mother's room when a nurse came in to adjust Mom's feeding tube. There was black stuff going through the tube and my sister asked what it was. The nurse said that it was bile; that mom's body was beginning to shut down, little by little, and that she would most likely pass in a day or two. She told us several other things very carefully and thoughtfully before she left. Although I heard my voice come out flat and hard as a rock, I thanked the nurse for explaining things so gently.

I remember half-heartedly doing a word search puzzle. Mom began to struggle for each breath and her entire body shook unnaturally. I couldn't look at her in this state. The body before my eyes was not the mom that I remembered in my heart. Then my little voice said, very clearly and very urgently, "If you are going to say good-bye to your mom, you had better do it now." I jumped out of my chair, startling everyone in the room as the word search book flew out of my hands and hit one of my nieces in the head. I sat next to my mom on her bed and held her warm hand. I kissed her face all over, much the way I kiss my children's faces. My last kiss was planted on mom's forehead. I told Mom I was going to miss having her in my life so much, and that I would always love her. She took her last breath when I finished my sentence. A warm and overwhelming feeling of peace poured over me like water.

I bowed my head and told God, "You gave me a gift today, and I need you to know that I really, really appreciate it. Your forgiveness knows no bounds. You took the beating that I gave you and gave me back unyielding grace. You gave me a heads up all day today and then allowed me to say good-bye to my mom. Thank you for loving me unconditionally."

As time goes by, I find that I miss my mom in spurts. One night, while rocking my second child to sleep, I found myself missing Mom something awful. On that particular day, I had wanted to call her with two history questions, and I needed baby advice. That night when I went to bed, I asked God to let Mom know that I love her and miss her so much, and that I could really have used one of her hugs that day.

That night, God bestowed yet another gift to me. I dreamed I was coming home from college and walking toward the house where I grew up. I leapt up the slanted stairs in my usual fashion and Mom answered the door, wearing her familiar muumuu and a big smile. She hugged me so hard I felt her heartbeat, and I could smell her scent mixed with the smell of fresh tortillas and beans from the kitchen. When I woke up, my eyes were filled with tears of joy.

Kristina's Angel

Theresa Hammerquist

"... It is not for you to know the times or periods that the father has set by his own authority. But you will receive power when the Holy Spirit has come upon you...."   — Acts 1:7b-8a

I pray that the God of our Lord Jesus Christ, the Father of glory, may give you a spirit of wisdom and revelation as you come to know him, so that, with the eyes of your heart enlightened, you may know what is the hope to which he has called you, what are the riches of his glorious inheritance among the saints....   — Ephesians 1:17-18

The year after our relocation from Canada to New Berlin, Wisconsin, was extremely difficult for everyone, particularly our four-year-old daughter, Kristina. During our first year in New Berlin, it wasn't uncommon to hear her say, "Nobody likes me. Everyone hates me." All of that would change during a sudden illness that scared all of us out of our wits.

One week before school started in August, 2000, Kristina, awoke early on a Wednesday morning complaining of a headache and fever. It struck me immediately that it could be meningitis, and since she is not one to complain about ailments, I gave her Tylenol, called my mom, who is an RN, and waited for the fever to go down. Later the same morning, she had the same complaints and needed to vomit. Following a mother's instinct, I took her to the doctor, who completed a thorough neurological exam to eliminate bacterial meningitis. Satisfied, I took her home.

Two hours later, I was on the phone with my sister. At the beginning of the conversation, I recall watching my daughters as

103

they played "dress-up." Just as my sister and I were finishing our conversation, Lexie, our oldest, came to tell me that Kristina's head was hurting again. I remained on the phone for a few minutes longer, hung up, and went to Kristina's room.

I was horrified to find her on her bed, purple in color and choking on vomit in her mouth and nose during a seizure. I tried to clear her mouth, but was unable because her jaw was locked from the seizure. I carried her to the kitchen, called 911, and prayed a simple prayer: "More time, she's only four." Lexie ran to tell the neighbor. We were on our way to the hospital via ambulance before I knew it.

When we arrived at the hospital, Kristina was disoriented but otherwise seemed fine. The contrast between the horrible sight in the bedroom and watching the chatty little girl in the hospital pajamas was simply unbelievable. Of course, we didn't know just how unbelievable until weeks after the incident.

Upon discharge from the hospital on Wednesday, she was diagnosed with a febrile seizure. Two days later, on Friday, we returned to Children's Hospital where Kristina was diagnosed with viral meningitis.

The day following her seizure, I took Lexie aside while Kristina played within hearing range and said, "You are a hero! You saved Kristina's life yesterday when you came to tell me that her head hurt. She could have died if it hadn't been for you."

Having heard our conversation, Kristina interrupted and began to flit around the room saying, "But, Mom, I wanted to die, I wanted to fly with the angels!" I distinctly remember, on that same day, as she descended the stairs, Kristina said in a cheerful, exuberant voice, "Mom, everyone loves me. Especially God, he really loves me!" Just days before she had been saying: "Nobody likes me. Everybody hates me." I knew then that God had acted in her life.

Days followed that were filled with similar inspirations from our four-year-old. I didn't know the degree of divine intervention, but I knew I was thankful to God for giving us extra time with her.

A month later, we had a get-together at our house. One friend who came had had a near-death experience during a routine tonsillectomy when she was four years old. Knowing Kristina had been ill, she sensed Kristina's lingering fear and told her she did not need to be afraid. I cherish her words, for they released the miracle.

The evening of the get-together, Kristina sat in the armchair alone and sobbed releasing her fears. I asked, "Why are you crying?"

She replied, "I was afraid when she left."

"When who left?" I asked.

"When the angel left my room to get Lexie to tell you that my head was hurting again. Then she came back and I felt better."

I felt a need to talk to Lexie immediately, to discover her memory of the event. I took her aside separately and asked, "Do you know anything about an angel?"

"No," she replied.

"Where were you when you came to tell me Kristina's head was hurting again?"

"I was in my room, in front of my mirror, putting on a necklace," she said.

I asked, "How did you know Kristina was sick again if you were in a different room?"

"Oh! Yes!" she replied. "I *do* know about an angel! When I met it ... I mean when I felt it ... I had it in my mind that I needed to tell you about Kristina."

I asked, "How did you know it was an angel?"

She replied, "I was in my room, standing in front of the mirror, putting on a necklace when I felt it. I felt a small wind. I know a fan wasn't going. I knew something or someone was there telling me about Kristina. It was in my mind to tell you." When we talked about the incident, she distinguished the angel as Kristina's angel, not her angel. She was very particular about this point.

The power of God and his messengers is unbelievable! I pray that God will keep the memory clear in our minds so we never forget the awesome blessing he gave us on that ordinary Wednesday in August.

Pentecost

I'd been lying in bed, and then this alternate reality took hold: I had this vision that Jesus was pouring water down this huge incision in my spine, and he said, "Your sins are forgiven." And I thought, "That's not what I want to hear," and I said, "Am I also cured?" and he said, "That, too."

Reynolds Price

Reynolds Price, *A Whole New Life* (New York: Atheneum, 1994).

Wrapped In Pentecost

Kate Jones

To each is given the manifestation of the Spirit for the common good. (v. 7)

When my grandmother, Virginia, died I wore a red dress to the funeral. It is not my habit to wear red dresses to funerals, but this dress is special. Grandmother Virginia and I bought it two years ago when I was visiting her in Tulsa, Oklahoma. We felt very naughty out shopping for the dress. My Auntie Dumpling left strict instructions: "Don't baby your grandmother." I didn't. It wasn't babyish to me to take her to the mall — a place she hadn't been in years. Auntie Dumpling didn't think my grandmother was up to such adventures. But, Auntie Dumpling was out of town! I tried on every red dress in the mall. Miss Virginia told me the story of how she eloped in a red dress while we rested on the brocade loveseat at a high-end department store. We watched mothers of brides in dress-buying rituals try on all manner of pastel dresses and suits while very young looking women scowled at their mothers' selections. We found the perfect dress, on the clearance rack: a tailored wrap around in United Methodist flame red, with a black and white polka-dotted lining.

I packed that red dress for a visit with Grandmother Virginia last March. I put it on for church and when she saw what I was wearing, she went back to the bedroom and put on her red dress. My ever perfectly coiffed, impeccably dressed grandmother insisted that I put on red lipstick — a very different look from my usually naked face — and we were off to stir up some trouble at the retirement center Sunday worship. We sang at the top of our voices in our outrageous red dresses. Early the next afternoon, I held Grandmother in my arms for the last time and said good-bye.

When I saw my dad's number on the caller ID at 7 a.m. on Monday morning, I knew. The lovely Miss Virginia, as her aids called her, had been called home. Again, I packed the red dress. I looked through the black things hanging in my closet, clerical collars, clergy suits, and my basic black dress. "No," I thought, "This is my grandmother's funeral. My red dress would somehow fit into her 'all things decently and in order' Presbyterian rubric." Since she had been a prominent member of the largest Presbyterian church in Tulsa for more than fifty years, I was certain that her pastor would officiate. At most, I would read the passage from Ecclesiastes about how there is a season for everything, or maybe tell a story about Miss Virginia. "Yes," I thought. "I'll wear red."

We arrived in Tulsa late on Wednesday afternoon. Wednesday evening, Uncle Danny, Aunt Cocoa, Auntie Dumpling, assorted cousins, and my three children and I were having supper in the non-descript hotel restaurant. Auntie Dumpling said she had talked to grandma's pastor. She told him that our full-service funeral family of storytellers, musicians, clergy, and other bards would plan the service. All he needed to do, she said, was the homily.

We sat at a large corner table, waiting for the patriarch, Miss Virginia's first born, my father, the Reverend Dr. Bob, with his large frame, a mane of silver hair, and an imposing presence. We traded stories and laughed and cried as families do when they prepare to bury their dead. The patriarch finally appeared, almost as a ghost, hunched over a cane, praying, "O, Jesus, O-O-O, Jesus" with every step. It jolted my grieving heart. I couldn't tell if it was my heart or his body breaking as he sat down next to me. Dad was in a lot of pain. "Katie, you plan and lead the service," he said.

The cadence of my heart hit double time as I contemplated the reality. My father just asked me to plan his mother's funeral. Here I was in the Bible Belt. Most of the worshipers would undoubtedly be high church, elderly Presbyterian ladies. I had no *Book of Common Prayer*, no robe, no clerical collar, no cross, and no stole. I had the small Bible I carry in my purse, my scrappy, Yankee, Methodist style, and a wrap around red dress, which would require a safety pin under the lapel if it were to be worn with modesty. Whether or not to select blood hymns was the least of my worries.

Uncle Danny picked up the tab and we dispersed. I retired to my room to make the collegial call to Miss Virginia's pastor. I got into one of those mazes of telephonic technology. After a series of numerical choices, I finally left a message for Dr. Johnson. I sketched out a service as best I could and then looked for sleep in the room I was sharing with my three children.

Funeral day came with the oppressive heat expected of any summer morning in Oklahoma. I once again tested my skills in the telephonic maze of the Presbyterian church. This time with more success. Dr. Johnson's assistant informed me that the good doctor could not participate in the funeral, as his father had died during the night and he needed to be on an airplane for Nashville.

I hung up the phone and sat for a moment in the hotel version of silence. There was a knock on my door. I opened the door to find my brother Rick, holding two packages. "Andrea made these for you. I was going to wait until your birthday, but she said to bring them now." I invited Rick in. I tore through the first package which contained a large, soft blue-green prayer shawl. As I opened the shawl, out fell a slip of white paper. Its words were immediately familiar.

> *O Lord, you have searched me and known me. You know when I sit down and when I rise up; you discern my thoughts from far away. You search out my path and my lying down, and are acquainted with all my ways. Even before a word is on my tongue, O Lord, you know it completely. You hem me in, behind and before and lay your hand upon me. Such knowledge is too wonderful for me; it is so high that I cannot attain it. Where can I go from your spirit? Or where can I flee from your presence? If I ascend to heaven, you are there; if I make my bed in Sheol, you are there. If I take the wings of the morning and settle at the farthest limits of the sea, even there your hand shall lead me and your right hand shall hold me fast. If I say, "Surely the darkness shall cover me, and the light around me become night,"*

even the darkness is not dark to you; the night is as bright as the day, for darkness is as light to you. For it was you who formed my inward parts; you knit me together in my mother's womb. I praise you, for I am fearfully and wonderfully made. Wonderful are your works; that I know very well. My frame was not hidden from you, when I was being made in secret, intricately woven in the depths of the earth. Your eyes beheld my unformed substance. In your book were written all the days that were formed for me, when none of them as yet existed. How weighty to me are your thoughts, O God! How vast is the sum of them! I try to count them — they are more than the sand; I come to the end — I am still with you. O that you would kill the wicked, O God, and that the bloodthirsty would depart from me — those who speak of you maliciously, and lift themselves up against you for evil! Do I not hate those who hate you, O Lord? And do I not loathe those who rise up against you? I hate them with perfect hatred; I count them my enemies. Search me, O God, and know my heart; test me and know my thoughts. See if there is any wicked way in me, and lead me in the way everlasting. — Psalm 139*

I wrapped myself in God's knitted womb and sat down on the edge of the bed holding those sacred words of God's profound and pursuing love. Rick handed me another package. "Andrea just took up weaving," he explained. "She made this for you, too. Isn't it perfect?" The stole was purple on one side — the color of penitence, and preparation — the color of Advent and Lent. On the reverse, it was white, the color of death and resurrection. "Rick, it *is* perfect. I can't think of a more perfect gift. Tell Andrea I love it. Thank you."

Rick excused himself to get ready for the funeral. I laid the prayer shawl and the stole on the bed. I wrapped myself in the red dress, put on some red lipstick, picked up the stole and my Bible, and went to gather the children.

Like most families, we entered the service after the other mourners had been seated. "Old Rugged Cross" played on the old, bad, synthesized funeral home organ. Unlike most families, my dad and I took the officiants' seats in the front of the room.

Wrapped in my red dress, and the stole, white toward the congregation and purple toward my heart, I got up and proclaimed: "Jesus said, 'I am the resurrection and the life. Those who believe in me, even though they die, yet shall they live....' "

As the witnessing continued, my dad leaned forward with characteristic impatience and uncharacteristic anxiety. This time, I laid my hand on top of his very large, square, spotted hand. He turned his hand over and we sat together, palm to palm, wrapped in Pentecost.

God Created Death?

John Sumwalt

*God saw everything that he had made, and in-
deed, it was very good. And there was evening and
there was morning, the sixth day.* (v. 31)

It happened at a fifth and sixth grade church camp that I directed with my wife, Jo, at Pine Lake United Methodist Camp in
central Wisconsin, several years ago. The theme was "Partners in
Creation." There were about thirty children and eight adult counselors. Each night we gathered around the campfire for worship
and storytelling. I invited everyone to make up their own creation
stories to tell as we studied the creation stories in Genesis through-
out the week. Each night we closed with a litany based on Genesis
1. I would say, "In the beginning God created ..." and then I would
point to one of the children, who would fill in the blank by saying
something like "trees," for example. And we would all say, "In the
beginning God created trees, and they were good. *Very* good!"

The blank was filled in by lots of obvious things, like rain-
bows, water, air, people, puppies, grandpas and grandmas, and so
on. Near the end of the week, I told the campers the sky is the
limit, and that they could include silly things. We had great fun
saying "In the beginning God created 'mosquitoes,' 'oatmeal,'
'armpits,' 'broccoli,' 'prune juice,' and 'homework.' And it was
good. *Very* good!"

We went along like that, doing a mixture of silly and serious
things, laughing and praising God with much joyous banter, when
I pointed to a little girl who had not said much all week, and she
said, "Death" (we discovered later that her grandmother had died
just before she came to camp). There was a poignant pause, a holy
hush as we looked around at each other, wondering if we could go
on with the litany. It seemed like a long time. but it was only an

instant, one of those moments that cannot be measured in time, when the Spirit moved in and through us, and we all knew that what the little girl said was true. We joined our voices together as one in a holy affirmation I will remember till my dying day. "In the beginning God created death, and it was good. Very *good*."

Sufficient Grace

Joyce Schroer

*God is our refuge and strength, a very present help
in trouble. Therefore we will not fear....*
— Psalm 46:1-2a

*To one is given through the Spirit the utterance of
wisdom, and to another the utterance of knowledge according to the same Spirit....*
— 2 Corinthians 12:8

A few weeks ago, I had a most unsettling dream. It awakened
me in the night and I could not go back to sleep. I dreamed that I
was sitting on a creek bank, with an unidentifiable friend, and we
were chatting, when suddenly I looked down to see an adder's den
below our feet. I started to jump up, but the snakes had crawled up
into our clothing and jackets. They frightened me, but not one of
them bit me.

I awakened and thought, what a strange dream. I ought to call
my friend Mindy (who was always interested in dreams) and see
if she can help me understand the meaning. Of course, by morning, too many other things were on my mind and I did not give
Mindy a call.

Two nights later, I had another unsettling dream. This time I
was swimming. The water was murky and I felt something around
my legs. Through the murky water I could see a huge sea creature.
I jumped out of the water and onto the bank just in time, again
without injury.

I awakened and thought, another strange dream! I really do
need to call Mindy. Once more, I was too busy the next day to
follow through.

Several nights later, I had a third unsettling dream. This time I was in a large house. It had many rooms and I was part of a procession. There were six of us, walking from room to room in a most orderly fashion. We were carrying bowls of Jell-O. As we neared the screen door, one person turned and exited, and the screen door slammed shut.

I awakened. I lay in bed and wondered, what do these dreams have in common? I thought and thought. Then I prayed, "God, I don't understand what these strange dreams mean, but if you have a message for me, please make it clear. You know that I can be rather slow and dense." Nothing came as I waited for God to speak to me. Then, before drifting off to sleep, the verse "My grace is sufficient for thee," came to my mind. I thought, "Okay, and thanks God, but I still don't understand." "My grace is sufficient for thee." I did not sense that I was going through a time in my life that I needed reassurance of God's grace. I decided I had waited long enough. I definitely needed to call Mindy.

Mindy has been one of my prayer partners for over ten years. There were six of us that covenanted with one another and we met weekly for study and prayer. Over the years, we became a very close-knit group of friends. Each one of us was different and we all had different gifts. I appreciated Mindy's gift of insight and her expertise when it came to dream interpretation.

I called Mindy first thing in the morning. She answered and I started with the formalities ... "Hello, how are you?"

She said, "I'm dying!"

"What? Dying?"

Mindy proceeded to tell me that had I waited ten more minutes to call she'd have been on her way to the hospital. Her cancer was back, it had snaked its way all through her body. The tumor was so large it changed the shape of her body such that she looked distorted ... the treatment she was scheduled for was so severe that the last time she'd had it, she nearly died.

I told her that I thought I had a message for her from God, "My grace is sufficient for thee." I cried, told her how much I loved her and that she'd be in my prayers. Then I proceeded to look up 2 Corinthians 12:8. I have not had any unsettling dreams since.

High And Lifted Up

Laurie Woodard

No distrust made him waver concerning the prom-
ise of God, but he grew strong in his faith as he
gave glory to God, being fully convinced that God
was able to do what he had promised. (vv. 20-21)

The story I am about to tell didn't seem to lend itself to words, due to the profundity of its content, and for many years it stayed in my treasure box of memories as an ethereal moment in my journey.

The Lord has shown great favor upon my husband and me. After two years of infertility procedures, we were able to conceive our first child. Our healthy little daughter didn't come into this world without a struggle. We never ceased to be grateful through-out prolonged efforts to lull her to sleep. As amazing as her life was, three years later she was joined by a sister who arrived with-out excessive waiting or complications of any kind. Number two daughter came with an even sleep pattern, which helped to restore my faith in motherhood.

About two years later, my husband announced that our family of four seemed incomplete, and that we should consider a third addition. I resisted that proposal for months because I really thought we had our hands full. But the Lord had other plans. He revealed them to me, one summer day, as I was riding my bicycle home from a Bible study titled, "The Challenge Of Being A Woman." The lesson of that day focused on the husband and his leadership role in the family. It suddenly became clear that God was asking me to yield to my husband's desire to expand our family.

My willingness brought us to a place of bounteous blessing, threefold! Not only did God send us a son, but two daughters to accompany him. In just six years, I had delivered five babies: two daughters born in separate births, followed by a triplet birth; two more daughters and a son! As a monumental number of feedings and diaper changes went by, and the purchase of a bigger residence came to pass, the rigors of parenting multiples continued, but not without God's constant provision and guidance.

However, nothing could have prepared me for the next event, a fourth pregnancy to top things off. I constantly asked, how could I ever carry another baby with my daily duties of tending to a kindergartner, a three-year-old, and three eighteen-month-old toddlers?

Every day was a physical and mental challenge. I continually battled feelings of anger, doubt, blame, desperation, and fatigue. How could I possibly complete this pregnancy and accommodate another baby? After about six weeks of sheer mental torment, I finally surrendered to God's will and agreed to accept my sixth child and trust God to make a way where there seemed to be none.

Shortly after my relinquishment, I was put on bed rest due to some moderate bleeding. After a weekend of lying in the horizontal position, I really expected everything to be fine, but the ultrasound told otherwise. The doctor announced that I had miscarried. While his condolences were sincerely extended to my husband and I, a sense of relief consumed me and I felt a flood of God's divine deliverance take over my entire body. Perhaps I had passed a test? Maybe God had no intention of continuing the burden of a pregnancy?

Although I cried no tears of sorrow, I had been given a temporary gift of a new life that I look forward to meeting in heaven. The ultimate reward was the incredible manifestation of God's love that entwined itself around me in a vision of being literally lifted up out of my bed. It seemed as if I was viewing myself, floating above the space where I actually was. Great torrents of God's merciful love swept over my body until I was overcome with a sense of being "high and lifted up." I can now truly say, "How great is the steadfast love of my Heavenly Father!"

I Gave You To God

Andrew Oren

*The Lord said to Abraham, "Why did Sarah laugh,
and say, 'Shall I indeed bear a child, now that I
am old?' Is anything too wonderful for the Lord?
At the set time I will return to you, in due season,
and Sarah will have a son."*
— Genesis 18:13-14

*"For this child I prayed; and the Lord has granted
me the petition that I made to him. Therefore I
have lent him to the Lord; as long as he lives, he
is given to the Lord."*   — 1 Samuel 1:27-28

My wife's cousin is Sister Joan Brede, a School Sister of St.
Francis, who recently celebrated her fiftieth year in the Order. As
I was preparing a sermon about Hannah and Samuel one day, I
thought of Joan and what her parents might have thought about
her decision to enter the convent. I asked her if she would share
with me what that time was like. She laughed and then told me a
remarkable story.

Joan was an only child of Dorothy and Charles. Her mother
was a devout Catholic, and one day, when Joan was twelve years
old, her mom came home from church and said to her, "Joan, I did
something today that has me a bit scared and I need to tell you
about it." Joan asked her mom what she had done.

"I gave you to God ... in prayer."

Joan, being twelve, didn't think much about it at the time. Joan
attended Pius High School in Milwaukee, and when she was a
junior, she felt a call to enter the convent. She told her mother, but
swore her to secrecy because she felt that if her father knew, he
would tell everyone and then she would have no social life! She

wanted to enjoy her last years of high school, so she waited until graduation to tell her father that she wanted to become a nun. Her father's first words upon hearing her decision were, "Where are my grandchildren going to come from?" Despite that initial hesitation, Joan's parents supported her and at the age of eighteen she entered the convent.

Well, imagine everyone's surprise when her parents announced soon after that they were expecting! Expecting a second child eighteen years after their first one! They had a son, and one day he did present them with grandchildren. Now, over fifty years later, Joan has touched countless lives through her work and faith.

A Doula's Prayer

LaNette J. McQuitty

Give ear, O Lord, to my prayer; listen to my cry of supplication. In the day of my trouble I call on you, for you will answer me. (vv. 6-7)

As a birth doula, I often find myself praying for my clients long before their labor begins. This particular time, for some reason, my prayers seemed to be much more intense. I prayed all week for a miracle birth, but you never know how God will interpret your prayers.

Labor for this mom, a first timer who wanted to go "all natural," began on October 23, 1999, at 6:30 a.m. She said she had things to do and she would page me when the contractions picked up.

She went about her business and paged me at 2:00 in the afternoon. I went to her house and, at about 4:30, off we went to the hospital. When we arrived, she was dilated to only two centimeters and decided to go in the Jacuzzi for an hour and a half. When she got out of the tub she was at four centimeters and we celebrated. I said more prayers, thank God!

The contractions really picked up and we spent the next two hours on the floor on our hands and knees together, then the deep squats started and I knew this was it. She was so beautiful, she just let her body lead the way. At 8:11 she said, "I can't do this anymore. I'm going to die."

I prayed and told death, *"No!* There is no way!" I had her checked and she was completely dilated. The baby was born at 9:12 p.m. and the doctor did not arrive on time. She nursed the baby and I stayed with her and prayed and thanked God for this beautiful miracle. Little did I know!

I got home at 1:30 a.m., still on a "high" from the birthing experience. My sister, who was watching my children, was just hanging up the phone. She turned to me and said, "Michael (my eighteen-year-old son) was in a severe car accident, ejected from the vehicle, and his neck is broken in two places. Flight for Life is taking him to Froedert Hospital and we need to go."

My heart was broken. I prayed the Our Father the whole way to the hospital. It was an hour before the helicopter landed, and much longer before the neurosurgeon told me that my son's spinal cord was ninety percent compromised. The damage was so severe that we should expect him to be a quadriplegic with only eye movement. His injury was similar to Christopher Reeves'.

They called in the best surgeon in the country and he arrived at 6:00 in the morning. He told me that Michael was lucky to have survived the accident at all. According to the reports, the first call for help came in at 8:11 p.m. (when the mother I was helping through labor said she was going to die), and four emergency departments from surrounding counties searched a cornfield for my son with no luck. At 9:02 they called for a Theda Star helicopter with an infrared heat seeking device, and that helicopter located him at 9:12. He was "born again" at the same time as the delivery I was attending.

I continued to pray throughout Sunday while they gathered up eight neurosurgeons to operate on Monday. I stayed in the intensive care unit at Michael's bedside the whole time, and when they took him for surgery he looked at me and said, "Mom, when I flew from the car I was caught by an angel, and God was with me the whole time I laid there unable to move." He said, "Call my friends and tell them I'm going to be fine." After ten-and-a-half hours of surgery (and we thought labors were long!), and two hours of recovery, the intensive care nurses said we could see him. They could not explain it, but Michael was moving his hands and feet and responding to touch.

Three days later my son was transferred to the Acute Spinal Cord Injury Center, where they had him take his first steps. They were a little slower than the first steps he took when he was ten months old, but they were no less important. The Flight for Life pilot came to his room and broke into tears. Michael was the only airlift that "made it" the whole week. They put him in a wheelchair, took him up to the roof and took pictures of him by the "ship."

Michael is known as the "Miracle Kid." He is at home now, and doing most things for himself.

A Cup Of Coffee

Tom Kadel

*Whoever welcomes you welcomes me, and who-
ever welcomes me welcomes the one who sent me
... whoever gives even a cup of cold water to one
of these little ones in the name of a disciple —
truly I tell you, none of these will lose their reward.* (vv. 40, 42)

I want to tell you about something that happened while I was
in Ohio, in July of 2003, just after my mother's death. It is a story
that involves a cup of coffee, a duck, and a toothless old man.

On the Tuesday following my mother's death, there was the
usual flurry of activity — people to call, arrangements with the
funeral director, planning the service with the pastor, and time with
family just remembering. Things went well, by the grace of God.

I was staying in a motel in Troy, Ohio, only minutes from the
hospital Mom had been in. I had been to Troy, but hadn't ever
really seen this beautiful little city. So, after all was done, and I
had said good-bye to my sisters and their families, I decided that
rather than go back and sit in the motel alone to await my family's
arrival the next day, I would just drive around and look at Troy.

But, there was something I had to have first — a cup of coffee
to take with me. Right next door to the motel was a little restaurant
called Crazy H's. To put the best light on it, we could call it "unas-
suming." It is the kind of restaurant where you always check your
silverware and plates to make sure that they've been washed —
you know the kind I mean.

I walked in and went up to the counter, where I was waited on
by a smallish woman with rather sunken features. "Hard Life"
was written in the deep lines that etched her face. She was probably in her forties, but could easily have passed for sixty. "May I

have a cup of coffee to go, please?" I asked. "Sure," she replied. After hunting for a cup and lid, she poured the coffee and handed it to me as I handed her my money. "Ah," she said, "forget about it. Just do something nice for someone."

She said that with a warm smile that overcame the deep lines in her face. I thanked her and left. As I drove away, I sipped the coffee. I want to tell you, it was the best cup of coffee I've ever had. It wasn't because of the taste. It wasn't because I got a freebie. It was because the coffee had the flavor of grace in it.

Maybe if this had happened on any day other than one so filled with emotion and meaning for me, I might not have tasted the grace. But that day, I did. I was truly moved, and I savored that coffee, sip by sip, as I rode around Troy viewing the city and thinking about Mom. I really wanted to find someone to be nice to, but since I didn't know anyone in Troy, I had no idea how that would happen. So, all by myself, I savored this cup of coffee, flavored with grace.

Grace is always undeserved. Grace is always a surprise. Grace is always one other thing, too. It is always something that has the power to transform us into persons we could not otherwise be. When that waitress said, "Just do something nice for someone," she transformed me into a person who truly wanted to touch someone else's life with an undeserved and unexpected measure of grace. But alas, I saw no one else that night.

The next day, there was practically nothing to do but wait for Thursday's funeral service. My family had left Harleysville and was on its way to Ohio. I decided that this was a good time to drive to my hometown, Urbana, and immerse myself in memories of Mom and Dad and friends and experiences that had shaped me. I was still thinking about that waitress' kindness as I drove the 45 minutes from Troy to Urbana.

My first stop was the city park — a place I just love. There is a big pond there with a tree-filled island in the middle and dozens of waterfowl — three or four swans, many Canadian geese, and dozens of Mallard ducks — all swimming peacefully. It was a good place to begin my memory tour.

As I watched all those birds float gracefully on the pond, I suddenly became aware of a flurry of activity about a quarter of the way around the pond. I couldn't see clearly what was happening, except that about a dozen ducks seemed to keep flying hard into another duck. I noticed *that* duck wasn't moving — just flapping its wings frantically. What could this be?

I began to walk over to that place and, as I drew closer, I noticed that the unmoving duck had its beak straight up in the air. Closer in, I could tell it was hooked on something. Closer still, and I could see that it was hooked on a fishing hook and the line was snagged in a tree. The duck was truly stuck and the others, with all their bashing and bumping, were trying to free it. But, the duck was caught.

I looked around, realized I was the only person in the park, and wondered what to do. I didn't have a knife and I didn't have a clue how to free the duck. It was awful to see. I bent near the spot where the captive and its friends were and tried to speak comfortingly to the terrified duck. I wanted so much to free it, but I couldn't. All I could do was try to soothe it.

"She's in a fix, eh?" The words from behind me startled me. I was sure I was alone, but suddenly there was this toothless old man in a kind of golf cart. I have no idea how I could have not heard him approach.

"Well," he said, "let's see if we can help." He had a knife and, remarkably, he had a small pair of wire cutters on his belt. Together we tenderly pulled the duck from the water and he cut the line and then removed the hook from the duck's bill. Even more tenderly, he placed her back in the water and she swam off, surrounded by the other ducks, to the far side of the pond.

"Hey," said the toothless old man, "that felt good, didn't it?" He laughed a bit as he watched the duck swim away. Then he called off to that duck, "Hey, Mrs. Duck, you go on and do something nice for another duck, okay?" My breath stuck in my throat.

As he started to drive off, I thanked him and he replied, "Oh, it's what I do. I work here."

I suddenly caught on. My experiences Tuesday night in Crazy H's and Wednesday morning at the park pond were not two events, but one — a story to comfort me and to teach me.

I had been approached by God in a hard-life-faced waitress and in a toothless old man.

I was as helpless against my mother's death as was the little duck against the fish hook. But that is when God provides. In our weakness, God's power shows through. In our weakness we are met unexpectedly by God who carries us through and saves us from our own powerlessness.

A cup of coffee, a duck, and a toothless old man. God was there. And now there is a certain duck and a certain man who know better than before that we cannot save ourselves, but that we don't need to. "Oh, it's what I do," says God. "I work here."

Is God Listening?

Barbara Frank

Come to me, all you that are weary and are carry-
ing heavy burdens, and I will give you rest. (v. 28)

My sixteen-year-old son had a very difficult time in the years following his father's death. Counseling, from many sources, was of little help. School didn't seem important to him. His friends were few, and the ones he had were not the ones I would have chosen as good influences.

One evening, as I waited for him to come home from his part-time job, I saw him go behind the garage with a friend. After a few minutes, I followed. I found them smoking what I thought, from the smell of it, was marijuana. After breaking up their "party," I called my older son. He searched his brother's room and found more marijuana and drug paraphernalia.

I was in denial. Not my son! He comes from a good Christian family. I would have known if such things were going on in my house. He is just having a difficult time. This is the kind of thing that only happens to other people.

What a wake-up call!

After a day of soul searching, prayers, and tears, I reached a decision. I had my son arrested.

Going to bed that night, I had second thoughts. What had I done? I prayed to God to please help me. In the darkness, a dim, distorted figure appeared; a presence. I had the feeling of arms surrounding me. Although I was responsible for this decision, *I was not alone.* God was listening!

My son had a few rough years, but today he has become a wonderful, responsible, and loving person, of whom I am very proud, and for whom I thank God every day.

A Light To My Path

Linda Willis Harper

*Your word is a lamp to my feet and a light to my
path.* (v. 105)

I was 27 years old and very active in our United Methodist
Church. I had taught Sunday school, been on the administrative
board, was president of the United Methodist Women, and sang in
the choir — maybe not all at the same time, but I spent enough
time at church to feel it was a second home.

One weekend, our church held a lay witness mission. Layper-
sons came to share their faith with us. One wonderful man who
was a witness stayed in our home. I knew, from the first time I met
him, there was something different about Don. He had something
I lacked and wanted. All the years of service in my church had not
brought me satisfaction.

On that Sunday, we were invited to come forward to the altar
and accept Jesus as our personal Savior. My friend and I came
down from the choir loft and knelt to pray the prayer of salvation.
I didn't see or feel any "special effects." I just made a choice —
the best one of my life. That was November 20, 1972, the same
day our new friend, Don, had accepted Jesus years before.

My husband bought me a Living Bible that day. I began reading, devouring, the scriptures. I couldn't get enough of the Word.
Later, I recognized this as the work of the Holy Spirit.

A few weeks later, I began to have doubts about my salvation.
I asked God for reassurance — a sign — and he gave me one I
shall never forget. As I was reading his Word, Ephesians 2:8-10
leapt out at me. I saw the words as big, bright, and bold as a neon
sign. The small letters of my Bible were replaced with inch high
ones so I could not miss the message. It said that I was saved by

grace, not by works, so I could not boast. God taught me, instantly, that his grace saved me, not all of the volunteer work I was doing.

God is so gracious to give us what we need, when we need it, as we trust him.

A Father's Love,
A Mother's Good-bye

R. Ellen Rasmussen

*I consider that the sufferings of this present time
are not worth comparing with the glory about to
be revealed to us. For the creation waits with eager longing for the revealing of the children of
God....* (vv. 18-19)

Even in the darkest of moments, the power of love can shine
right through, crossing galaxies to calm and soothe. Here is one
daughter's experience.

My father died four days before Easter, 1995. He was a good
man, a kind man, a man of justice. Through his death, I experienced wailing and truly knew what it felt like to lose a part of my
very being. I eventually realized that, because I could feel such a
deep loss, I could also feel deep love.

Dad's death caused me to flashback to my high school years,
when he worked nights and would always check to make sure I
was home and in bed when he got home. Often, he would sit at the
end of my bed and we would talk about what had happened that
day, what was going on in school, whatever. The rest of the house
was quiet, and Dad and I would talk. As I look back now, I see
how wonderful and special that time really was.

During December of 1995, my mom had been ill. I finally got
her to the hospital and had her admitted because she was dehy-
drated. I found out that morning it was more than that. As I walked
into my mom's hospital room, I heard her doctor say, "It looks
cancerous. We'll know more when we operate tomorrow." Without missing a beat, I continued to walk to my mom's bed and sit
down. She didn't want anyone to know. It was our first Christmas

without my dad and she didn't want my brothers and I worrying about her. The tumor causing an obstruction was small and they hoped to remove it all. I spent the day with my mom and then went home to make arrangements for my children to be with someone else so I could be at the hospital during her surgery.

That night I had a visit from my dad. Sitting at the foot of my bed, he was so real. His voice was so clear, and his eyes were filled with love. He told me, "Ellen, I know that you are going to do the best for your mom and I know how much you love her. Remember that I love her too, and I am waiting for her. I will take care of her when you no longer can." I woke up. I knew my dad had been there and I knew my mom was dying. I knew I didn't have much time. That was confirmed the next day. The surgery took longer than anticipated, and they said the tumor had already metastasized to her liver and lung. Later, I would learn that we had about six months, and that's just what we had.

My mom spent her last six months trying to get everything in place — making sure my brothers would be okay, making sure that her mom was in an assisted living situation, making her funeral arrangements, making notes at work for the one who would replace her — trying to make sure everything was just so. The last 36 hours were pretty rough. She didn't know who I was and kept calling me "Grandma Gray." She wanted me to make the pain go away. I was caring for her at home, and I had reached a point where I needed to get some sleep. I couldn't keep going, but she needed someone by her side. I finally convinced one of my brothers to come over.

I went downstairs to my room and tried to get some much needed sleep. I closed my eyes and all of a sudden my mom was at my doorway, just like she used to appear to get me up for school. In all of our conversations about everything, we had never talked about me. She asked me if I was going to be okay. I told her that I loved her and that I would miss her very much, but yes, eventually I would be okay. My mom left. I woke up with a start and bounded up the stairs. I ran past my startled brother, who asked what I was doing. I said, "Mom needs me." He said, "She's sleeping."

I lost Mom on May 10, 1996, the Friday before Mother's Day. I was blessed to share her final moments. I was able to hold her and tell her how much I loved her and how much I would miss her. She died in my arms, but I knew my dad and God were waiting for her, and that she went from one set of loving arms to another. She just had to wrap up that one loose end before she could go.

Praying: Even When You Can't

Pamela J. Tinnin

Likewise the Spirit helps us in our weakness; for we do not know how to pray as we ought, but that very Spirit intercedes with sighs too deep for words. And God, who searches the heart, knows what is the mind of the Spirit, because the Spirit intercedes for the saints according to the will of God. (vv. 26-27)

The year I turned forty, I spent my birthday at a three-day women's retreat. The retreat was held at a Catholic boarding school. None of us knew each other, so it was a bit awkward that first night, especially when it came time for bed — six women, all ages, sleeping in the narrow cots of a dorm room.

By the second night, after a day of study groups, worship and prayer, silly skits and games, and eating three meals together, we were old friends. It was more like the slumber parties I remembered from high school — lots of giggling and whispering long after "lights out." After a while the voices faded away one by one, until the room was quiet except for the sound of soft snoring.

I lay awake a long time, thinking about the events of the day — the sight of eighty women, all ages, shapes, and sizes, trying to hold balloons between their knees as they raced, or more accurately stumbled, to the finish line; the words of every old camp song I'd ever learned sung by eighty adult female voices of every description; the flicker of a hundred candles in a darkened chapel, the light gleaming on the bowed heads around me.

In those three days, we prayed a lot in groups, the prayer moving from one to another around the circle. The retreat leaders prayed for us, sometimes with tears on their faces. We even had a midnight prayer walk, each of us holding the hand of the person ahead and behind, with only the team leaders holding a flashlight. I tried to concentrate, to "clear" my mind and heart and reach out to God with fervent words, but all I could do was concentrate on not falling, wondering what the dark shadows were and where the path would take us.

Prayer has never come easily for me, public prayer in particular. Instead of just speaking from the heart, sometimes I get hung up on whether I'm going to sound stupid, or whether my prayer is going to be "good enough." In fact, I usually write out a public prayer rather than risk making a mistake, saying "the wrong thing."

However, not long ago, I learned something important about prayer. I was at the local hospital visiting a church member, an elderly man who was there following surgery for a broken leg. I saw a young man in a wheelchair, so thin his face wasn't more than a skull with skin stretched tight and marked with numerous small bruises. I'd seen him before over the past few years, enough that I smile and nod and he does the same. He had never spoken, but I couldn't help notice that each time I saw him, he was thinner, his eyes sunken deeper in dark circles, his bony hands trembling more and more.

This time he reached out and touched my arm. "You're a pastor, aren't you?" he asked me, his voice a husky whisper. "The lady at the counter told me — my name's Robby."

"Yes," I answered, telling him my name and that I was from Partridge Community Church.

"I'd like you to pray for me," he said, his words coming out slow and awkward. "I'd surely appreciate it. I wouldn't bother you, but ... see, I've ... I've got AIDS ... don't have much time left."

Not knowing what to say, I looked around. I think I was hoping for some other pastor to come along, someone to bail me out, someone who could pray eloquently and powerfully. There was only a young woman pushing a cart stacked with meal trays, a gray-haired couple who got off the elevator laughing at some private joke ... and me.

My own voice took me by surprise. "Yes, Robby, I'll pray for you." And I did — right there in the hallway. I leaned in close so

136

he'd have no trouble hearing, put my arm around his shoulder, took a deep breath, and prayed that the right words would come. I thanked God for loving Robby, for being there to help him not be afraid. I asked that Robby be forgiven for any sins and that he be able to forgive anyone who had hurt him in his life. I prayed that Robby would find comfort and feel at peace in the hard days that lay ahead of him.

I don't know how long we stayed there, our heads bowed, then I said, "In the name of the Risen Christ, Amen." When I looked up, there was the young woman who had passed by earlier. She stood against the wall next to the stainless steel cart, her head bowed. When she opened her eyes, she smiled at us, mouthed the word "thanks," then patted Robby's knee and pushed the cart into the waiting elevator. Tears were streaming down Robby's face even though his eyes were shining and he was smiling this enormous smile.

Last week Robby's mother, whom he hadn't seen in nearly ten years, came to take him home to Texas. I pray that whatever time they have will be blessed.

Like that prayer walk I took some fifteen years ago, at times our lives can follow dark and shadowed paths to places unknown. The only light may seem far away and out of reach. But, like I told that young man in the wheelchair, there isn't one of us who isn't a beloved child of God — beloved. When we pray, there are no mistakes, no way to "say the wrong thing." In fact, if we can't find words, we can just wait without speaking, assured that the One who loves us can hear the silent yearnings of our hearts.

Too Churchy

Paul Karrer

When he went ashore, he saw a great crowd; and
he had compassion for them and cured their sick.
(v. 14)

The doctor had never been to Kenya before and to say he was overwhelmed didn't begin to hint at his inner turmoil. Five chiropractors from four corners of the United States had volunteered their time, all costs, and expertise for two weeks. They had been sponsored by a church organization and for "Jake" it seemed just a little too churchy.

They stayed in a colonial-era hotel that separated them from the locals. But each day they went to "the tent." A white tent, open on all sides, welcomed in all of Africa's ailing. At least it seemed that way to Jake.

"There are at least 2,000 of them," he stated incredulously to one of the other doctors, and he was correct. Outside in the sun, beneath the pepper trees, an army had appeared. They had heard the news — free medical care by American doctors. So they stood in the burnt brown grass waiting for their turn at the benches. Jake used a simple wooden bench and under the head of each patient he placed two books to lift their necks — the Bible and Margaret Meade's *Coming of Age.* Jake, like the other doctors, did quick assessments of the patients before him. Then he began his adjustments. But a few thoughts lingered ... *these people are really ill. Some of them suffer from more than one ailment. Some are HIV positive, and I'm giving them ADJUSTMENTS! But maybe, I'll help just one. What else can I do?* Each day he and the others worked for hours. Once a fight broke out. Too many needed care.

This went on for seven days. On the last day, Jake, hammered physically, and emotionally, let off some steam by wandering in

138

the street market. Soon he felt a tap on his shoulder and turned to face a man.

"Doctor, doctor, please look at me."

Jake turned. "Oh, no," he thought, "I can't do any more."

A muscular Kenyan man faced him. "Look what you did." The man radiated a smile. "I don't need my cane. I can stand straight."

Jake thought he recognized him, but there had been so many.

"Doctor, I have something for you. I have looked for you all over this town." He unfolded a piece of paper and handed it to Jake. It was an old newspaper article.

"That was me. I ran in the Olympics for Kenya. I couldn't stand for twenty years. Now I don't need a cane. Here, you keep this article. I signed it for you."

Jake accepted the gift and he didn't know what to say, but he did know what to think. "Maybe it wasn't too churchy. I asked for one and you gave me one — thanks!"

Angels In Haunted Places

Richard H. Gentzler, Jr.

And early in the morning he came walking toward them on the sea. But when the disciples saw him walking on the sea, they were terrified, saying, "It is a ghost!" And they cried out in fear. But immediately Jesus spoke to them and said, "Take heart, it is I; do not be afraid." (vv. 25-27)

My interest in angels began rather abruptly one sunny, summer afternoon while visiting Hershey Park, in Hershey, Pennsylvania. "Let's go into the Haunted Fun House," I suggested gleefully. Although I had never been in a Haunted Fun House before, the bright lights of the marquee intrigued me. "No," came the quick response. None of my family members, including my parents, aunts and uncles, and grandparents had any desire to enter a "Haunted" Fun House. I whined and pleaded with them to let me go in by myself. "No, you're too young," they retorted. "I'm big enough to go by myself," I implored. And, like many a young boy, I pestered them until they finally gave in.

Perhaps you have experienced the joys and delights of a Haunted Fun House. I didn't. This Fun House was not fun at all. At seven years of age, I found the Fun House dark and scary. When I entered through the doorway, I could see nothing. Nothing, that is, except pitch-blackness. Suddenly the door shut and I stood inside, alone. I tried taking several steps, but I could not see a thing. My eyes had not yet adjusted from the bright daylight to the complete and utter darkness of the room. My heart started racing. I was overcome with great fear. I could not find my way through the dark maze. I was alone and very frightened. Soon I began to whimper. My eyes filled with tears and I started crying, uncontrollably. I couldn't see. I couldn't move. I was frozen in utter darkness.

Then, an angel appeared. Not that I could see the angel, but a hand reached out and grabbed my hand. The angel whispered assuringly, "Don't cry, little boy, everything will be all right." And it was. The angel's voice was so reassuring and comforting that I quickly stopped crying. Before I knew it, the angel led me through the dark maze of the tortuous "Fun" House.

When we exited the building, I wiped the tears from my eyes. The angel, still holding my hand and walking next to me, was a teenage girl. She was a stranger to me, but she was my angel. She had led me safely through the unknown, and reassured me with her voice and gentle touch. Angels come in all sizes and ages and places. Sometimes, angels even come to little boys in dark, fearful Haunted Fun Houses.

A Time To Weep

Christina Berry

Then he fell upon his brother Benjamin's neck and
wept, while Benjamin wept upon his neck. And he
kissed all his brothers and wept upon them; and
after that his brothers talked with him. (vv. 14-15)

A dear friend's eldest son, age 31, died unexpectedly in early
June in a city on the West Coast. As she and her husband were
planning to travel there, from Arizona, to attend a memorial service his friends and partner had arranged, and to collect his things,
she told me that her husband did not know their son was gay. The
relationship between father and son had been strained in the past,
and we were sure her husband, a really traditional guy, would not
handle this information well.

"How could he not know?" I asked. "Are you going to tell
him?" She said she would wait and see.

They had so much to deal with in their preparations that we
never had a chance to talk again before their trip. Amidst much
chaos and grief, they left home.

On the plane, she said something in passing about their son
and his roommate. Her husband answered, referring to the roommate as their son's partner.

My friend said, "Where did you learn that?"

"Well, he told me."

"What did he say?"

Her husband related what their son had told him.

"When did you find out?" my friend asked, shocked.

"Two years ago, that time I was in the hospital."

"Why didn't you say anything to me?"

142

Her husband looked surprised. "Didn't you know?" he asked. She was so relieved she didn't have anything more to say.

When they arrived at the home of their son's friend, where the memorial service was being held, the first person they saw was the son's partner. My friend said her big, macho husband looked at this bereaved young man, went to him, enfolded him in his arms and said, "Thank you for loving my son." And the two of them wept together.

Help In The
Name Of The Lord

Sandra Herrmann

Blessed be the Lord, who has not given us as prey
to their teeth. We have escaped like a bird from
the snare of the fowlers; the snare is broken, and
we have escaped. Our help is in the name of the
Lord, who made heaven and earth. (vv. 6-8)

In 1972, I had the opportunity to go to the Soviet Union and get educational credit for the adventure. The University of Wisconsin at Eau Claire had built a class around the travel event, teaching us a few words of Russian ("Excuse me," "Where's the bathroom?" "How much does it cost?" and so on), an outline of Russian history, some exploration of the current culture, and the basic tenets of Communism, as we would see it. The trip to get into the Soviet Union was exhausting, especially since a man in our group turned out to be smuggling letters to families from their relatives in America, and we were held for hours while our bus was searched and all of our luggage gone through. It was not a gentle introduction to the Soviet Union, and some of the excitement of being in such a strange place was drained out of me.

The next few days were spent in sightseeing, and having the opportunity to meet fellow students at the University. My attitude toward the Soviets was on a rollercoaster. We learned how much they had suffered in WWII, and that they had lost most of their young men in that conflict. All of the rebuilding that took place after the war had been done by unskilled laborers, men and women, under the direction of the few men remaining who had been trained in architecture, mixing of concrete, and bricklaying. Many of the buildings showed that they had been built that way, with cracking concrete, crumbling cement and mortar, and a gray sort of look.

But the pride and joy of Leningrad is their subway system. It was not a good place to build such a system, because the city had been built, 200 years previous, on a marshland. Rocks and boulders were the tax that had to be paid by every peasant and craftsman bringing work into the city to sell. The rocks had been dropped into the swamp until it was firm enough for buildings to be erected.

In order for the subway to be built, they had had to go down to the bedrock underlying the swamp, and the erection of a ceiling and walls was more of an effort than I could imagine. They took such pride in the result, that they had painted and tiled the various stations as beautiful works of art. So, of course, the students we met wanted to know what we thought of the subway. We had to admit that because there were so many of us in the tour group (seventy all together) we had taken ground transportation. The last night we were in Leningrad, a student we had met two days earlier met us at our hotel to take us to a club downtown. We would, he announced, take the subway.

But when we arrived at the station (having walked a mile in a snowstorm to get there), it was packed with people! "It's the end of the weekend," he said. "Everybody likes to go to the country to visit, and now they're all coming back. It will be okay. Just look for the sign overhead, you will see where the escalators are. I will meet you at the bottom if we get separated."

I was in a panic. I hate escalators. They are one of the few things that truly frighten me. When I was a child, I'd had an accident on one, and I had always been afraid of them since. The only other thing I dislike is a crowd, and this was a crowd the likes of which I had not seen in my life, not even when I had visited in New York City! How could I do this? Worse, I *had* to do this, because I had no idea how to get back to the hotel by myself. Besides, I really wanted to enjoy this evening with the very friendly student who was disappearing into the crowd as I watched.

Trembling with fear (I had never been so afraid, I was certain!) I did as he had instructed, and aimed for the sign that pointed downward. But when I got to the top of the escalator, I found that

145

I couldn't see the bottom! Nor could I possibly stop at the top, as I usually do, to be sure my foot is on the tread and not the crack. Suddenly, someone grabbed my arm, and said, "Don't be afraid. I have hold of you. Just step when I tell you. Now!" and I stepped forward, onto the tread, and safety.

I took a deep breath, and in gratitude turned to thank the woman who had helped me. But in that crowd, the only people close to me were men, except for a little babushka (grandmother), who clearly did not understand a word of English. For it was in English that I had been addressed, and as I thought about it, Midwestern English, at that — no hint of an accent of any kind to my ears. Bewildered, I turned around and scanned the crowd, but no one returned my glance.

The next day, I told others in my group about the experience. One of the men offered the observation that many Russians were learning English, and they perhaps didn't want others in the crowd to know this. But, I knew this did not explain my adventure. I knew that no one near me was tall enough to have grabbed my arm the way I was grabbed, and none of them would have sounded like a woman from my part of the world. But there is One who speaks our language always, and who has said, "I will give my angels watch over you, lest you dash your foot against a stone" (Psalm 91).

Response

Marie Regine Redig

There the angel of the Lord appeared to him in a flame of fire out of a bush; he looked, and the bush was blazing, yet it was not consumed. Then Moses said, "I must turn aside and look at this great sight, and see why the bush is not burned up." When the Lord saw that he had turned aside to see, God called to him out of the bush, "Moses, Moses!" And he said, "Here I am." Then he said, "Come no closer! Remove the sandals from your feet, for the place on which you are standing is holy ground." (vv. 2-5)

In the summer of 2003, I was yearning and hungering to deepen my relationship with God in an intimate way, so I took a week away to pray in the country at a lake. On the fifth day I was sitting by the lake when the words came to me and they flowed from my pen as the tears rolled down my cheeks. This is what I heard and what I said in response:

Knock!
Yes?
It's Jesus and I've brought my Father with me.
Welcome!
We want to make our home with you.
Not much here but what I have is yours.
It's enough!

The Winds Of God

Larry Winebrenner

Owe no one anything, except to love one another;
for the one who loves another has fulfilled the law.
(v. 8)

My grandmother was an unforgiving woman.

She lived on a farm in South Carolina, with a peach tree in the backyard. When any of her children, a couple hardly older than me, or any grandchild misbehaved, she grabbed a switch from that peach tree and peppered welts on our little legs for the transgression. It didn't matter whether the act was deliberate or an accident — out came the peach tree switch. There was no escaping it.

One day I accidentally (and carelessly, I might add) knocked her favorite tea pitcher off the kitchen table and broke it. My grandmother was out taking the slop to the pigs, but not for long. I could hear her coming up the back steps to the porch, which was just outside the kitchen. There was no escape that way. I knew some of the family were in the living room and would see me fleeing out the front door, so there was no escape that way. I was still small enough to crawl into the cabinet under the sink, so I quickly jumped in there and closed the door.

Just in time! I heard my grandmother shriek when she walked into the kitchen. She set the slop bucket down and screamed, "Who broke my tea pitcher?"

There was a trampling of feet as everyone in the family came scrambling into the house. There was a chorus of "Not me," "It wasn't me," "I don't know," and the like. Then came those dreaded words as Grandmother said, "Where's Larry?"

My heart sank. I was really in for it. No one knew where I was, and at that moment, I wasn't about to tell.

"Go find him," commanded Grandmother. "Edna, go get a new switch off the peach tree."

Boy, was I in for it. I shriveled up into myself, trying to make myself small enough to crawl out through the mouse hole in the wall. I hardly breathed. To make it worse, Grandmother didn't leave the kitchen. She went on preparing supper while the family went out looking for me.

The first person to report in was Carroll, an uncle a year older than me, and normally a staunch companion and playmate. Grandmother on the war path broke down all alliances. He had searched diligently for me, whether to warn me or to rat on me, I didn't know, but I suspected that in the light of Grandmother's demands it was the latter.

"Mama," he said. "I've looked everywhere he might hide and I couldn't find him."

I had to struggle to keep from snickering.

"Keep looking," she demanded, and he went back out. Gradually others came in to report. "He's not out in the toilet," Robert said. All we had was an outdoor privy, and that's what he was talking about. "He's not out in the garden or chicken house," said Edna. To each report Grandmother gave the same command: "Keep looking."

Meanwhile my legs began to cramp and my feet went to sleep. When Granddaddy came home from the field down the road and on the other side of the pine woods, she asked, "Did you see Larry on the way home?"

"No. Why? Is he lost?"

"More like hiding," said Grandmother, and she explained what happened.

"Well, let's eat. He'll be home for supper, I'll guarantee that. That boy eats more than any two grown men I've ever seen. I don't know why he's so skinny," said Granddaddy.

"He eats so much it makes him poor to carry it," Grandmother observed as she went out on the back porch to ring the dinner bell.

When everyone came in, each reporting no luck in finding me, she said, "Wash up and get ready for supper." To Edna she said, "Set the table."

The back porch was closed in and a table for regular meals was out there with a bench on each side for the kids and a chair on each end for Granddaddy and Grandmother. When they were all seated and Granddaddy had said grace, they started eating. There was no conversation about me because it was a firm rule that you didn't talk about anything at meals.

Once, when my father was visiting for Sunday dinner, he chatted away like he was sitting in the parlor. I thought Grandmother was going to run out and get a peach tree switch, but she only glared at him.

In my hiding place in the kitchen I could hear the rattle of dishes, the clink of silver on plates, the sound of Granddaddy smacking as he chewed with his mouth open. We were always told to "chew with you mouth closed" by Grandmother, but she never told Granddaddy that. The smell of collard greens, pork chops, gravy to go on the rice, homemade pickles, sliced tomatoes, and everything they were eating wafted through the closed door. My belly gurgled so loudly I was afraid they'd hear it.

After supper, Granddaddy spoke. "Robert, you and Carroll go milk the cows and take care of the animals. Annie (to my grandmother), let the dishes go for now. It will be dark before long. You and me and Edna better go look for Larry. If he didn't answer that dinner bell, he's sure lost. He may have fallen in the old well or gotten lost in the woods. We've got to find him."

For the first time I heard a note of concern in my grandmother's voice. "I don't know what's gotten into that boy. Yeah, we better go look for him."

Even though the house was empty, I didn't dare come out of my hiding place. To my young mind I suspected this was a ruse cooked up to get me to reveal myself. Before long I dozed off.

Suddenly, I awoke with a start and hit my head on the sink. "Mama!" Edna was yelling. "He's here, under the sink!" I didn't know how long I'd slept — it was pure dark outside — but I knew the time of judgment had come. Grandmother grabbed me by the shoulders and dragged me from under the sink. She picked me up like a rag doll and shook me till my teeth chattered.

"Why did you scare the life out of us like that?" she cried.

150

When she quit shaking me enough that I could speak I said, "I was afraid you'd kill me for breaking your old tea pitcher and I didn't have any way to run away."

She looked at me in shock and set me on my feet. My legs were still asleep and I collapsed to the floor. She didn't pick me up. She just looked down at me. "Honey, I'd never kill you," she said softly.

I knew I was as good as dead, so I spoke my mind. "Yes, you would. When you get mad all you think about is yourself. You care more about that old tea pitcher than you do about me."

She looked at me a minute, then fled to her bedroom. Granddaddy picked me up and took me out to the table. All the food was still there. Edna had been looking under the sink to get the dishpan, so nothing had been done yet to "rid up" the table. Granddaddy put a big pork chop on my plate and some rice with collard greens on top the way I liked to eat them.

"Eat something," he told me. As I sat munching on the food, he talked to me.

"Annie doesn't hate you, boy. She loves you like one of her own children. If she punishes you, it's the same way she punishes her own children. She does that to make you good." He thought a moment as I chewed the last bit of meat off the bone and wiped my mouth on my shoulder sleeve. I reached for another chop. I didn't mind that they were cold. I love pork chops. He continued, "You know why you come stay on the farm every summer? It's because you're so wild your mother can't handle you. Now I don't mean you're bad wild. And I don't mean your mother doesn't love you."

"I know," I said. "Mother loves me very much. She tells me that all the time."

"Well, so does your grandmother. And she wants everyone else to love you. That's why she works so hard to make you good," he told me.

I'd never heard my grandfather talk so gently and so kindly. I looked carefully at him to see if he was putting on an act prior to slapping me from the table, but no, he was earnest. I saw tears glistening in his eyes.

151

"My grandmother hates me," I said without malice, but with conviction.

"Have you ever heard your grandmother lie about anything? Ever?"

"No," I said.

"Then, go in there and ask her if she loves you," he said. It was not a command, but it was a direction that was not to be disobeyed.

I jumped down off the bench, wiped my hands on the seat of my pants, and marched myself into her bedroom. She was lying face down on the bed, sobbing uncontrollably.

"Grandmother," I said tentatively.

She rolled over and sat up on the edge of the bed. She wiped the tears from her eyes with the corner of the sheet, but they remained red and swollen.

"Do you love me?" I asked.

She burst into tears again and clasped me to her breast, almost squeezing the breath from me. "Yes," she said, "Yes. Yes, I do. When I thought you were lost all kinds of fears raced through my mind. What if you were kidnapped? What if you had gotten lost in the woods and were hurt and scared. What if you ran away and were lost to me forever. My heart was breaking."

"Why are you crying?" I asked.

She took my shoulders, held me out in front of her and looked me in the eye. "When you told me that I loved that tea pitcher more than I loved you, I realized there was a little bit of truth to that. I didn't really love it more than I loved you, of course, but I realized I loved things. Yet, people are so much more important than things. I just hadn't thought about that. I knew it must look to you like I loved that pitcher more than I loved you. I couldn't stand it. I love you. I want you to know I love you."

Then she asked me a question that shook me to the roots of my soul. "Do you love me?"

I didn't know how to answer that. I had never thought about that. Did I love my grandmother, the one who cut peach tree switches to wear out on me? I saw the tears welling up in her eyes as I struggled with the question. I wasn't going to lie to her. I might say, "I don't know," or "I'm trying," but that wasn't the question. The question was, "Did I love her?" All at once a kind of light dawned. What hurt me most when she punished me was my fear that she didn't love me. That wouldn't matter unless I loved her. But now she was telling me forthrightly that she did love me. I didn't have to worry about that any more. My grandmother didn't lie. Ever.

"Yes," I said. "I love you very much."

We hugged, and she cried, and I cried.

The revelation that each of us experienced was like the wind of God blowing over becalmed waters to billow sails and move the mighty Cutty Sark. It was like a gentle breeze wafting through the sun-drenched garden and over sweat-drenched bodies, bringing relief and comfort. The Spirit of grace entered that little house in one tiny corner of the world, revealing the source of all love.

My grandmother still switched me when I misbehaved, but I always knew it was to make me good so people would love me.

Louise

Kay Boone Stewart

The angel of God who was going before the Isra-
elite army moved and went behind them; and the
pillar of cloud moved from in front of them and
took its place behind them. It came between the
army of Egypt and the army of Israel....
— Exodus 14:19-20a

"I will sing to the Lord, for he has triumphed glo-
riously; horse and rider he has thrown into the
sea. The Lord is my strength and my might, and
he has become my salvation...."
— Exodus 15:1b-2a

Louise Martin is a marvel.

Born prematurely, she was accidentally dropped on the floor by a nurse shortly after birth, and death seemed imminent. So sure was the physician, that the birth registrar was sent away, and it was not until she was grown that Louise had a birth certificate. Birth was her first miracle, but not her last. You see, God had work for Louise.

This petite, silver-haired lady with sparkling eyes has lived through more miracles than most people can imagine. After a severe illness during which she had a near-death experience, Louise had a vision from God that she felt was leading her to leave her life in California and do his bidding.

Another miracle followed her survival, in the 1930s, when she was traveling to Harlem, New York, to see about working with the International Peace Mission. Those traveling with her had been "called" to this country from other parts of the world, feeling led by the Spirit to work with the disenfranchised. They were from India, Africa, France, Germany, and the United Kingdom, with a fair number of people of color in their group.

Once enrolled at the Mission, this select group would scatter to different parts of the U.S. to work with inner city problems and other needs involving people, performing both long- and short-term ministries.

While motoring toward New York, the seating on the bus was arranged according to sex. Women sat together and men sat together, which meant that Louise, a Caucasian, was seated next to an East Indian woman. The group had made a pact to never be separated for any reason in the interest of their ministry and safety.

As they entered Georgia, the bus was stopped by a patrolman who told them they would have to change their seating. When they refused, he told them the Ku Klux Klan was waiting for them around the next corner.

The bus proceeded, and sure enough, the Klan accosted them, demanding that the driver get off the bus. The Klan told him everyone must change seats, with all the Blacks in the back. The bus driver said they wouldn't, and he turned to re-board the bus. Strangely, the handrail was so *hot* he had to cover it with his cap to climb back on. He locked the door behind him.

The Klan made a run at the bus with weapons in their hands. An invisible shield stopped them from approaching the bus. It was as if they hit a wall when they ran toward it. They toppled over one another and landed in a heap, still brandishing shotguns and swords.

The bus driver hit the accelerator and sped away. The group proceeded on their way, giving thanks for the timely and amazing intervention of God.

Worth Waiting For

Ruth F. Piotter

*For to me, living is Christ and dying is gain. If I
am to live in the flesh, that means fruitful labor
for me; and I do not know which I prefer. I am
hard pressed between the two....* (vv. 21-23a)

One day, exactly ten months after my husband, Paul, died, I
was standing in an open area outdoors and saw three figures approaching me, walking very briskly. When they got closer, I recognized them to be Paul and both of my parents. My father died in
1937, my mother in 1966. My father had white hair, but was very
spry, and my mother now had dark hair, which I hardly remember
her having. Paul looked like he did when he was ready to play
tennis in college. They wore regular clothes, but had new bodies
unencumbered by any physical problems.

Paul spoke first, in his own voice, and said, "Do you have
your pass?" I said I had nothing and then all three said, "It is well
worth waiting for. Your new place is not quite ready for you and
you have some unfinished work left to do here, but when that is all
done, we will come back, take your hand, and walk with you to
the new place that is well worth waiting for."

They turned and walked briskly into the most beautiful sunset
of red, blue, purple, and gold, and into a golden tunnel of light. I
so wished I could have gone along right then. I felt exhilarated,
yet relaxed, as if completely at peace. I wish I knew what it is I
need to finish so I can get my "pass."

Nothing In My Brain

Cindy Loomis-Abell

Let the same mind be in you that was in Christ Jesus, who, though he was in the form of God, did not regard equality with God as something to be exploited, but emptied himself, taking the form of a slave, being born in human likeness. (vv. 5-7a)

My eight-year-old son, Jeremiah, has endured several medical problems. The one constancy among these problems was two kinds of seizures that caused difficulties for him in everyday life. Jeremiah has never known life without seizures, so he takes them, and the difficulties they cause, in stride. Three years ago, his father and I received the news from an MRI scan that new problems had come to light. The two abnormalities, which doctors were certain would increase in size as Jeremiah grew, would most likely require surgery.

This past spring, another MRI was done, and Jeremiah and I went to the neurologist for the results. He understood that a bad report would probably mean surgery and a hospital stay. He held my hand as the doctor came into the room to give us the news.

"Well, young man, I have good news to report. Your MRI was clean. There are no abnormalities in your brain. You have nothing to worry about!" he said with a grin, and accepted my child's happy hug.

As we walked to the parking lot, Jeremiah let go of my hand and skipped along, singing in a loud voice, "I have nothing in my brain! I have nothing in my brain!" all the way to the car.

Older people smiled and laughed. Mothers with young children smiled. When we got home, we all celebrated. For once, there was nothing but God's love in Jeremiah's brain. All of the abnormalities had mysteriously vanished.

I am absolutely certain that God has a special plan for this child. Wouldn't we all like to look like a clean MRI — no darkness, no hatred, no anger — only happiness and lightness of being? Wouldn't we like to live as real children of God, just as Jesus suggested? He said, "Let the children come to me. For to such belongs the kingdom of God." I hope we all find a way to have "nothing" in our brains someday!

Looking Forward
With Love

Lois Ann Weihe Bross

... this one thing I do: forgetting what lies behind
and straining forward to what lies ahead, I press
on toward the heavenly goal for the prize of the
heavenly call of God in Christ Jesus. (vv. 13b-14)

This story is very difficult for me to tell. It happened shortly
before my father's death. He had been in the hospital — dying, we
all knew — after a series of massive heart attacks. There was almost nothing left of his heart and he was barely alive. The doctors
had done everything they could for him. It was hard to understand
what was keeping him going, and even harder to watch him suffer
so terribly.

My husband, Ed, and I drove down from Milwaukee on a beautiful morning in May — the eleventh to be exact — my mother's
birthday, to spend the day with her and Dad. Ed's parents were
planning a birthday dinner that evening. When we walked into the
hospital to see Dad, we found that he was quite agitated. His heart
was in rough shape, but there was certainly nothing wrong with
his brain! He fully realized that it was Mom's birthday, so he had
been planning a mission for me as a part of what he wanted to do,
in her honor. He sent me to the Hallmark shop down the street to
pick out a card, such as he might have chosen, so that I could bring
it back for him to sign, and we could deliver it to Mom that evening.
Of course, Ed and I did as he asked, then returned to his hospital
room and propped and arranged him so he could sign the card.
This involved a great effort on his part, since he was so very weak.
In the process of helping him, I didn't see what he wrote, and, in
fact, it was quite some time before I saw it. However, I did read it

before he died. What he wrote to my mother, and really to all of us, was, "Looking Forward. With Love, LeRoy."

When I finally did see his message, I didn't understand it at all. I was not ready to say a final "good-bye" to my father. My first reaction to his statement, therefore, was that he was telling us that he was "looking forward" to getting well and doing all the things he loved to do — walking his dog, fishing up at the lake, and so on. I had to think that signature over for a long, long time, probably until at least six months after his death, before I began to understand what he was actually telling us. I finally realized that, above all else, my father was a man of deep and abiding faith. That birthday message to my mother, and to the rest of us through her, was his final statement of his faith to all of us. It was the shortest and yet the most profound sermon of his life.

Dad understood that his days and moments in this life on earth were limited, so he was preparing himself, and his family, for what he believed was coming — a joyful reunion in a beautiful place where the humiliation of pain and death would haunt us no more. Besides, my dad always did have to go on ahead, you know, to check things out. Even in heaven!

I still have my mother's birthday card; it is one of my most treasured possessions.

Inside A Tornado

Carolyn Peake

My soul magnifies the Lord, and my spirit rejoices in God my Savior, for he has looked with favor on the lowliness of his servant. Surely, from now on all generations will call me blessed; for the Mighty One has done great things for me, and holy is his name. (vv. 47-49)

Having been in the Protestant church all my life, I never gave much thought to Mary. She was just sort of the third person in a nativity set or someone revered by the Catholics. But I look at her very differently now.

I have been getting some counseling from my pastor (of the Northfield United Methodist Church in Vermont). Often, as we work on a topic, I will enter into a time of prayer and meditation to see what God wants to show me or tell me. In these times, it is not unusual for us to sense the presence of the Holy Spirit and/or angels.

But this time as I prayed, I felt another presence in the room. Pastor Ralph said, "Carolyn, who is standing to your right?" I knew who it was, but didn't want to put ideas in his head, so I said, "I don't know." Then, after a pause I said, "But it's a woman." And he replied, "It's the Blessed Virgin." I said, "Yes, it is." I knew it was.

The next night I spoke to him and admitted that I had lied when I said I didn't know who was beside me. He smiled and told me that he could see her.

She has continued to be with me, sometimes quietly and nurturing, sometimes with a bit more flair. One Sunday, as we were entering into the Eucharist time, for some reason I asked Mary if she would like to "enter into" me and experience the Eucharist with me. She spoke a quiet "Thank you," and suddenly I felt a sense of worship welling up in me like I have never felt before. It was impossible not to lift my hands in praise! Tears filled my eyes.

When it was my turn to kneel at the rail for Communion, I accepted it, crossed myself, and suddenly I felt like I was inside a tornado and it was inside me! I knew it was the Father, Son, and Holy Spirit! It felt "sparkly"— like the twinkling of a huge fireworks display without the smoke and noise! I was caught up in it, inside and out. I wanted to just stay on my knees. Words are just too weak a vessel to describe this!

Mary continues to be with me every day. For the first time in my life, I don't feel alone.

Is It Asking Too Much?

C. B. "Cleve" Bishop

*Moses said, "Show me your glory, I pray." And
he said, "I will make my goodness pass before you,
and will proclaim before you the name, 'The Lord';
and I will be gracious to whom I will be gracious,
and will show mercy on whom I will show mercy.
But," he said, "you cannot see my face; for no
one shall see me and live." And the Lord continued, "See, there is a place by me where you shall
stand on the rock; and while my glory passes by I
will put you in a cleft of the rock, and I will cover
you with my hand until I have passed by; then I
will take away my hand, and you shall see my back;
but my face shall not be seen." (vv. 18-23)*

They say you can't go home again, but I thought I'd try
anyway. I went back to Seattle to visit my stepfather for a couple
of weeks, after having been away for over twenty years. We
really did have a good visit and enjoyed one another's company
immensely.

One day, I decided to take the bus downtown, by myself, just
to wander around and relive the "good old days." What a shock! I
was amazed (and appalled!) at how things had changed ... in fact,
virtually *all* of my perceptions were so negative that I ended up in
a really foul mood. I then decided that the only way to work all of
the negative "vibes" out of my system would be to *walk* back to
my stepdad's place, even though it was over ten miles. This was a
natural decision for me, as I was "into" walking for my health, at
the time.

As I walked, I carried on a running conversation with the Lord:
"Lord God, I don't know what it's going to take to cheer me up!

I'm in a really foul mood, Lord! About the only thing I can think of that might cheer me up, Lord, would be to find a hundred dollar bill!" That thought stuck in my mind and I kept it up. "Lord, if I could find a $100 bill, it would be about the only thing I can think of that would cheer me up!" Grumble, grumble!

After a while, I was walking beside a chain-link fence that enclosed an Industrial Park, bordering a four-lane highway — no residences, no side streets, no cross streets, no chance of anybody ever finding *anything* along this stretch — and I *found* a $100 bill!

In Monopoly money!

I laughed right out loud and said, "Lord, you really knew what it would take to cheer me up!" I sang praises to my God all the rest of the way home, I *knew* it had to be the Lord's doing, because I have never before nor since found *any* denomination of Monopoly money!

I learned several valuable lessons from this: 1) God hears me. 2) God knows me better than I know myself. 3) God answers me. 4) God wants me to be *specific* when I pray (I had not specified a $100 bill in legal U.S. tender). And, best of all, 5) God has a terrific sense of humor!

Prayer At Midnight

Marjorie K. Evans

Let your work be manifest to your servants, and
your glorious power to their children. (v. 16)

One night, a number of years ago, I woke up with a start, almost as if someone had called me, and I sat up in bed. I saw that it was midnight and that my husband was sound asleep, so I lay back down. But as soon as I did, the name Addie Gordon popped into my mind, and I felt I was to pray for her.

Realizing it must have been the Lord prompting me to pray for Addie, I asked, "Why should I pray for her, dear Lord? I scarcely know her; I only met her once when she was home on furlough from her missionary work in Taiwan."

Then, I remembered the advice our Bible teacher had recently given us. She said, "When the Holy Spirit brings someone's name to mind, pray for that person. Pray specifically if you know the need. If not, pray that the Lord will meet the need the person has."

Still a bit puzzled, I prayed, "Dear Lord Jesus, I don't know Miss Gordon's need. But you know, so please meet whatever need she has. If she's ill, let her get well. If she's in danger, guard and protect her, Father, and keep her safe from harm. Amen."

After that, I felt at peace and was able to go back to sleep.

Several years later, Addie came home on furlough. At a luncheon, which our Bible club gave for her, I related the "prayer at midnight" incident to her.

Addie became extremely excited and asked, "When was that?" As we pinpointed the time, she said, "Oh, thank you! Thank you! Thank you! That was the time a terrible typhoon struck in the small city southeast of Taipei where our mission compound is located. It broke the dam, and the river began flooding.

"The river was only about 200 yards from my house, which began shaking around noon, midnight your time, as the water came in. I had no way to get to higher ground as the water was about three feet high and swirling and rising rapidly. I grabbed my small Bible, opened the top part of my door and called out, 'Chiu ming, chiu ming — save me, save me!'

"A young naval officer who often came to the compound to interpret for us had left a while before and was at a bus stop on his way back to the naval base. But suddenly he had a strong impression, 'God wants me to go back to the mission.' So he hurried back, heard me calling, and replied, 'I'm coming, Miss Gordon!'

"He quickly got a boat and rowed me to the top of the hill to safety. It took several weeks for the water to recede. When it was low enough that we could get into the house, we had to take my things out and dry them on the roof as the ground was still very soggy.

"Marjorie, I'll be forever grateful that the Lord awakened you at midnight and that you obeyed his urging to pray for me. I truly believe it was your prayer that saved me. So, whenever the Lord urges you to pray for someone, do it immediately!"

Stand Still And See!

Bonnie Compton Hanson

Let the redeemed of the Lord say so, those he re-
deemed from trouble.... (v. 2)

A few nights ago, I let our cat out, as usual, but I didn't see her come back in. "Don," I called, "have you seen Calico?"

You see, our cat loves playing her nightly watch-the-great-lioness-in-action game. Crouched behind a pot of flowers, she stalks her prey — then, *POW!* Of course, her prey's never anything more than a moth or cricket!

Soon, though, she usually tires of the game and is ready to leave her "wild side" for our warm, secure, cat-dish-furnished house! We're just as happy to have her as she is to have us. All my life I have loved animals of every description. Well, not snakes, maybe, but everything else, especially dogs and cats.

My husband glanced up from his books. "Didn't know she'd gone out."

"That's okay; I'll go bring her in."

Outside, a golden moon shimmered against the night sky. Crickets and tree frogs chirped. Somewhere in the distance, dogs barked. "Okay, girl," I called, "game's over. Come on out of your hiding place and get ready for bed."

Just then, two huge dogs came bounding down our street. Obviously they'd slipped off their leashes or broken out of their yards. Still calling Calico, I walked out to the end of our driveway.

Suddenly, out of nowhere, those two dogs hurled right up to our yard, stopping inches from me. One was a chow; the other, an ugly mixed breed with powerful, rippling muscles.

I expected them to wag their tails and whine to be petted. Instead, their eyes were glazed, their fangs bared. Both snarled as if ready to leap on top of me and finish me off right then.

167

I froze. The house was too far away for me to turn and run to it. "God, please help me!" I prayed silently.

Right at that moment, I distinctly heard a voice inside me say, "Stare at them! Don't lose control! Stand still and see the deliverance of the Lord!"

I was shaking so badly, I could hardly stand up. But I did stand. And I stared as hard as I could.

Snarling and snapping, the two dogs stared back. Then they turned as one and headed on down the street.

I let my breath out. Safe!

But instantly, they both whirled around and charged right back — leaping right up into the air in front of my face!

"Stand still!" commanded the voice. I was absolutely terrified, but somehow I kept standing and staring. And those dogs stopped right where they were. Right in midair!

Again they lunged — this time close enough for their spit to spray my face. But, again, an unseen hand held them up in midair and kept them from touching me.

They ran off, frustrated. But again, before I could even take a step back toward the house and safety, back galloped those same two howling monsters. This time, with a long, running leap, they hurled themselves at me with all their might.

Again, they were stopped right there in midair.

Finally, snapping and growling with disgust, they headed on down the street. And this time they didn't return.

No wonder poor Calico had been hiding! In fact, it took me a full hour of coaxing before the frantic cat finally streaked in through our front door. It took that long for my own shakes to subside, as well.

But not my praise to my Heavenly Father. For he had not only told me what to do when I was too panic-stricken to think for myself, but gave me abundant power to do it.

I did stand still. And I did see the deliverance of the Lord.

That You May Not Grieve

John Sumwalt

But we do not want you to be uninformed, broth-
ers and sisters, about those who have died, so that
you may not grieve as others do who have no hope.
For since we believe that Jesus died and rose
again, even so, through Jesus, God will bring with
him those who have died. (vv. 13-14)

Diane was eight years old when her brother Larry died. Larry was nine. They had always been close. Diane followed her older brother everywhere. They helped their dad and mom on the farm, cared for the animals, chased each other around the buildings, played hide-and-seek in the hay mow, and rambled through the meadow and the woods behind the barn. Diane would confess years later that she had been a bit of a tomboy.

One day, Diane was invited to go with two of her girlfriends to a baseball game. Larry asked to go along, but Diane said it was just for girls and they didn't want any boys tagging along. In the end, their parents decided that this time Larry would stay at home.

When they arrived at the game, there was a message that they should return home at once. Larry had been killed in a tractor accident. He was riding on the back of a tractor driven by one of the neighbor's hired men. The tractor had hit a bump, throwing Larry forward and down under one of the big rear wheels. His father, who was following behind on another tractor, picked him up and rushed him to the hospital where he died a short time later.

Diane's first thought was, "I'm all alone. I'll have to do everything by myself now." And then she felt a terrible, agonizing, painful guilt in the pit of her stomach. "If I had let Larry go to the game, this wouldn't have happened."

On the third night after the funeral, Diane wakened suddenly, sat up in her bed, and saw Larry sitting on the window sill across the room. Several moments passed as they sat there just looking at each other. "And then," Diane said, "Larry vanished right before my eyes."

When she told her family later, Diane said, "No one doubted me."

Diane says that she still gets goose bumps when she tells this story. She says, "To this day when I close my eyes I can see Larry sitting there just as he was that night when he appeared in my room."

If you were to ask Diane why she thinks Larry came to her, she would tell you, "I felt it was his way of saying good-bye, and God's way of showing me he is alive."

Editor's Note: Diane Henderson related this story to the editor in May of 1988. It appeared in *Lectionary Stories: 40 Tellable Tales For Cycle B*, John Sumwalt, CSS Publishing Company, Inc., 1990, pp. 77-78.

A Different Realm

Susan D. Jamison

*To you I lift up my eyes, O you who are enthroned
in the heavens!* (v. 1)

I've got rhythm running in my bones, in my blood, in my entire being — always have had. As a child I wanted to play the
drums, and my parents agreed to this because no purchase of an
actual drum was involved. In the fourth grade, I began taking lessons with a set of drumsticks and a drum pad (a small block of
wood with a rubber pad on the top). We had a very small band in
that elementary school, for it was a laboratory school held on the
campus of the state university in my hometown. I can remember
only one other drummer, a boy named Mark. When I entered the
public junior high I was not quite ready to be the only girl drummer in the entire school (this was back in 1971, before girls did
that sort of thing), so I played drums for the local majorette drill
team, which was just as well because I couldn't twirl a baton to
save my life. But I could bang on those drums in any pattern that I
was taught, and so marched in parades with a set of three drums
hanging from my shoulders. The high school drummer who taught
us encouraged me to play for the marching band when I entered
tenth grade, so I decided to pave the way as the first girl drummer
ever in the history of Indiana, Pennsylvania. I was not well accepted by the boys in the band, primarily because I was as good
as, or better than, most of them; not quite good enough to play a
snare drum, but good enough to play a tenor drum rather than be
stuck with the base drum that rarely varied in its beat. In concert
band, I played everything from tympani to snare drum, to maracas
and the triangle, and yes, even the base drum on one or two pieces.
The one thing I never did learn to play was a trap set. The cost of
one alone was enough to keep me from that.

171

I dropped out of the band for my last two years of high school because it interfered with my growing involvement in the church, first in my local church youth group, then at our United Methodist District and Conference levels. My passion for rhythm was set aside, buried in some ways, coming out only on the dance floor on the rare occasions that I had the opportunity to go dancing — didn't matter what kind of dancing: modern, country line, square, folk, contra, and even liturgical. As life got busier with seminary, marriage, children, and working, I had less and less opportunity to stay connected to the rhythm of life, and a part of me was dying inside. I just didn't recognize how much a part of me it was.

That began to change when I went to Kirkridge, a retreat center in the Pocono Mountains, for a weekend of dancing and drumming, in 1995. There I began to reconnect with my inner rhythm as I played drums for the first time in many years. The drumming leader was Montego Joe, from the Caribbean, who had drummed with The Fifth Dimension and for Alvin Ailey, among others. He had brought drums from Africa that are played mostly with bare hands. Because I was the only one in the group that had ever used drumsticks, he had me use them on certain drums. It was great fun and a real blessing to begin to uncover that rhythm that had been buried for so long. When I returned home I bought a frame drum, one that is held with one hand and struck with the other, either with an open palm or a beater (a stick with a leather cover on the end), and used it on occasion, mostly with a small group of women with whom I meet twice a month for spiritual support. I also went to a couple of workshops on drumming, but didn't really integrate drumming back into my life. Last summer, a friend — who was my son's fourth grade teacher, now retired — invited me to join a weekly drumming circle, but my pastor's schedule doesn't allow me many free evenings on a regular basis, so I declined.

Then, in the spring of 2003, I found myself once again at Kirkridge for an event called EarthCare, an annual weekend that includes things like cleaning up the grounds of the retreat center, clearing and marking trails, planting flowers, and picking up trash along the roadway. This year the facilitator was a woman named Elle, whom I had met about a year before through a mutual friend

172

in my hometown of Sunbury, and she brought with her an enormous drum she had purchased on a trip to Arizona. It was three feet tall and three feet in diameter and sat on a small pedestal. She knew I had some drumming experience, and invited me to play this magnificent instrument. I hesitantly picked up the two beaters and softly played, as we were in a rather small meeting room. Later in the evening as we did some simple circle dances for Universal Peace, I played again, keeping it rather soft to fit the mood. The weekend was wonderful, as it always is when I am at Kirkridge. As we gathered on Sunday for a closing worship, I was asked to play for about ten minutes to call us to worship, which was held outdoors. The drum was sitting under the large pine trees in the yard, and I approached it with great expectancy, for I would finally be able to play with abandon, as loudly and with as much energy as I could generate. During that time I was transported into a different realm as the Spirit's energy flowed through my arms into the beaters, changing from one pattern to another with no real plan but plenty of rhythm. Gradually, I felt as if I had become one with the drum, with the rhythm, with all of creation, and with God.

A Choice To Make

Susan Monnarjahn

Turn my eyes from looking at vanities; give me life in your ways. Confirm to your servant your promise, which is for those who fear you. Turn away the disgrace that I dread, for your ordinances are good. See, I have longed for your precepts; in your righteousness give me life.
— Psalm 119:37-40

For there is no distinction, since all have sinned and fall short of the glory of God....
— Romans 3:22b-23

It was only after a long tumble into the abyss of selfishness and self-involvement that I awoke to God's embrace of grace. If you have never reached the level of self-disgust that comes before a major rehaul of your life, you'll probably never comprehend the soul-shattering depths called "bottoming out." If you have been through it, then you are truly one of the blessed walking this earth.

The morning I had my vision happened after a long night that began with many fancy cocktails at a trendy dance club in Waikiki. It started, as many nights of drinking did for me at that time, full of glamour, high hopes of the men that might find me desirable, and the thrill of excitement. I made it home in one piece after a night of dancing and continued the drinking with a bottle of wine. In the beginning of a blackout, I decided that partying at a friend's house seemed like a good idea and didn't have any problem hitting the Hawaiian highways.

It wasn't the first time I had gotten behind the wheel in an alcoholic blackout. The police report said my vehicle had careened from one side of the three-lane highway to the other, until it finally collided with a barricade and came to rest on the grass. I came out of the accident with a badly bruised arm and an even worse attitude. After being booked with DWI, fingerprinted, photographed, and thrown in a cell, the fog started to lift a little. Sitting behind bars, humiliated, it dawned on me that I could be sitting here knowing that I had hurt or even killed another human being — maybe even someone's innocent child.

It was the first time I had thought of someone, other than myself, in relation to my alcohol use. That alone is miraculous.

My night of shame and degradation continued as I was hauled before a judge, dismissed, and thrown out the door in the bright, fresh, sunlit Honolulu morning. I politely asked the police officer at the door for change to make a phone call, and the look he threw my way shocked me. He didn't see anything but another pitiful drunk.

It was a busy Saturday morning downtown, with Japanese tourist groups adding to the regular local traffic. In my fog, I had thought I was on the other side of the island. Luck was finally on my side when I figured out I was only a couple of blocks from my place of employment. Walking disheveled, hung-over, and barefooted over the sun-baked tar was a brand new experience for me, and with every step my shame deepened. Could this really be happening to *me* ... a good girl from a fine family, neighborhood, and school, respectable in all ways, always?

Sneaking into the office without keys on a Saturday morning normally would have been impossible, but luck was on my side again as I found the cleaning crew had left the door propped open, allowing me to find a phone without attracting the undue attention of a few co-workers diligently toiling away that bright summer morning. The taxi driver agreed to accept a check for the ride home, as I had no money with me. My keys, along with my shoes, were still in the wrecked car, so my only alternative was to break a window to get into my house.

Finally, deeply shaken, I stood in my bedroom, almost in shock after the morning's ordeal. Could this horrible litany of events actually be part of my life? I barely recognized the woman, who earned the scornful stares of strangers as no better than any other street dwelling drunk. The constant throbbing of pain in my arm would not let me forget even for a moment what I had just endured.

As I stood looking toward the window, the sparkling waters of Pearl Harbor caught my attention through the curtains. At that moment, I saw my Creator, a strong presence of God, with both hands outstretched. He let me know that I had a choice to make in that moment, and I was not going to make it without the benefit of *his* vision.

On his left hand, he showed me how my life might progress if I continued to go down the path that I had chosen thus far. In a moment of vivid clarity, this presence granted me the insight to see exactly how selfish my lifestyle had become, and the true effect this self-centeredness was having on others. It was as if one moment I was blind to an entire aspect of truth and life, and in the next moment I could see everything clearly.

On God's right hand there was no picture that disturbed me. All I was being shown was *unknowing*. The Creator was saying that no outcomes are guaranteed, but to choose rightly would be to choose him. The decision I had to make, in that single moment, was to choose him with no promises or solutions, or to choose the path I had been on for so long.

Even without pictures to guide me, I felt that there was no way I could go back to my previous life. I knew without a doubt where that road would lead ... maybe I'd be a bag lady eventually. More certain was the fact that if I didn't change, I would be dead soon, or at the very least in prison, knowing I had caused the death of another. The vivid clarity I had been granted made my choice clear. I would choose God. I would choose to change my life by whatever means necessary. I would not look back.

Together Again

After this I looked, and there was a great multitude that no one could count, from every nation, from all tribes and peoples and languages, standing before the throne and before the Lamb, robed in white, with palm branches in their hands. (v. 9)

Barbara Frank

We got married young. I guess you could say we grew up during our years together. It was a good marriage, and we had three wonderful sons. During our 23 years together we enjoyed each other and our life.

After a long illness, my husband passed away. When his life ended, it seemed as if mine did, as well. I had a difficult time in the years following his death. I was so afraid of forgetting all of our memories.

One night I had a dream. It was the first and only time I had a dream about him. I was entering the gates of heaven, and God said to me, "He has been waiting for you." I didn't need to know anything else. I awoke with a smile on my face.

This is not the life I planned, but with God's help, it is a good and fulfilling life. As much as I miss this wonderful man, I know God has chosen the best.

We *will* be together again!

Bonny Joy Bailey

My "big brothers," Jack and Harold, were eleven and eight years older than me. When I was born, they told my parents to name me Joy because I gave them so much. But, of course, they didn't know what it was like to have a little baby sister. Time passed and we all grew up and had families. We all lived in the same city for most of our lives. My brother, Harold, had to move to Arizona because he had asthma. My brother, Jack, stayed here and helped my mom after my dad passed away. He was there for me also, when I went through a divorce and was raising four children on my own. I knew he loved me.

My kids grew up and I had a good job, so I was doing well on my own. We were not as close as we got older, but I knew Jack was always there for me. Mom passed away, my brother, Harold, died and left a hole in my life, but I still had Jack, quiet, strong, helpful, and loving. He was the only original family member left.

Then Jack developed congestive heart failure and ended up in a nursing home, where he stayed for a couple of years. He hated being there and told me he wished he could let go. His memory started going. He was a policeman and was very unhappy to have lost control of his life. He had six children and many grandchildren and great-grandchildren. When I got the call that he had been taken to the hospital and wasn't expected to live, I went to see him. He was unable to talk and just lay there. I told him I loved him and he should let go and go to God. Then I just sat there and held his hand.

On November 6, around 1:10 a.m., I got another phone call. My niece said the doctors did not expect Jack to make it through the night and if I wanted to see him one more time I should come right away. I thought about it and decided not to go. I went back to bed and lay there crying and asking God to be with him and his wife and all his children. While I lay there a feeling came over me. I felt a presence, as if I was being held and I knew it was my brother saying good-bye. I looked at the clock and saw that it was 2 a.m. Shortly after that, my niece called again to tell me he had died, but I already knew.

An Overpowering Light

Karen Steineke

I pray that the God of our Lord Jesus Christ,
the Father of glory, may give you a spirit of
wisdom and revelation as you come to know
him.... (v. 17)

It seems like a lifetime ago, because it nearly is. When I was 21, my husband and I chose to become members of the Wauwatosa Avenue Methodist Church. Neither of us had been members of a church growing up, only going occasionally with friends. For me that was extremely rare. I only went a few times. Our minister, Reverend Kerns, suggested that I be baptized, since I had no memory or record of having been baptized as a baby.

We set a date, and I remember being quite nervous, having no idea what it would be like in spite of the pastor's description of the ceremony. At that time, the chapel was a recent addition to the main building, along with Sunday school rooms. It was so like a dream, remembering it now, but one I recall totally.

As the pastor was performing the rite, I began to feel a warmth around me, all encompassing, with everything around me suffused and without form. I looked up to see the form of Jesus with an overpowering light surrounding him. For what seemed like minutes, I was suspended in time and space. I felt such love and awe. I remember my tears and, as we left the chapel, I tried to hide that from my husband because I was so overcome with a feeling one cannot describe.

Until years later, I never did tell anyone, but it has always been such a comfort to me, knowing that the Lord is with me. I know that many others have had similar experiences, but I feel so honored that it happened in my own life. I have shared it with close friends and family, but only those with a relationship with Jesus are receptive and seem to believe. Perhaps, the others are just unable to respond to such an amazing experience.

I don't care if you have seen the light, or felt the
magic; are you gentle, are you kind, when you are
stuck in traffic?

Christine Kane

Send your vision stories and other "shining moments"
when you have been in the presence of the holy to John
Sumwalt, 2044 Forest Street, Wauwatosa, Wisconsin
53213. Fax: 414-453-0702. E-mail: jsumwalt@naspa.net.
Phone: 414-257-1228.

Christine Kane, "The One Thing I Know," from the album
Rain & Mud & Wild & Green (Asheville, North Carolina:
Big Flat Music Label, February 19, 2002), track 11.

U.S. / Canadian Lectionary Comparison

    The following index shows the correlation between the Sundays and special days of the church year as they are titled or labeled in the Revised Common Lectionary published by the Consultation On Common Texts and used in the United States (the reference used for this book) and the Sundays and special days of the church year as they are titled or labeled in the Revised Common Lectionary used in Canada.

Revised Common Lectionary	Canadian Revised Common Lectionary
Advent 1	Advent 1
Advent 2	Advent 2
Advent 3	Advent 3
Advent 4	Advent 4
Christmas Eve	Christmas Eve
Nativity Of The Lord / Christmas Day	The Nativity Of Our Lord
Christmas 1	Christmas 1
January 1 / Holy Name of Jesus	January 1 / The Name Of Jesus
Christmas 2	Christmas 2
Epiphany Of The Lord	The Epiphany Of Our Lord
Baptism Of The Lord / Epiphany 1	The Baptism Of Our Lord / Proper 1
Epiphany 2 / Ordinary Time 2	Epiphany 2 / Proper 2
Epiphany 3 / Ordinary Time 3	Epiphany 3 / Proper 3
Epiphany 4 / Ordinary Time 4	Epiphany 4 / Proper 4
Epiphany 5 / Ordinary Time 5	Epiphany 5 / Proper 5
Epiphany 6 / Ordinary Time 6	Epiphany 6 / Proper 6
Epiphany 7 / Ordinary Time 7	Epiphany 7 / Proper 7
Epiphany 8 / Ordinary Time 8	Epiphany 8 / Proper 8
Transfiguration Of The Lord / Last Sunday After Epiphany	The Transfiguration Of Our Lord / Last Sunday After Epiphany
Ash Wednesday	Ash Wednesday
Lent 1	Lent 1
Lent 2	Lent 2
Lent 3	Lent 3
Lent 4	Lent 4
Lent 5	Lent 5
Passion / Palm Sunday (Lent 6)	Passion / Palm Sunday
Holy / Maundy Thursday	Holy / Maundy Thursday
Good Friday	Good Friday
Resurrection Of The Lord / Easter	The Resurrection Of Our Lord

Easter 2	Easter 2
Easter 3	Easter 3
Easter 4	Easter 4
Easter 5	Easter 5
Easter 6	Easter 6
Ascension Of The Lord	The Ascension Of Our Lord
Easter 7	Easter 7
Day Of Pentecost	The Day Of Pentecost
Trinity Sunday	The Holy Trinity
Proper 4 / Pentecost 2 / O T 9*	Proper 9
Proper 5 / Pent 3 / O T 10	Proper 10
Proper 6 / Pent 4 / O T 11	Proper 11
Proper 7 / Pent 5 / O T 12	Proper 12
Proper 8 / Pent 6 / O T 13	Proper 13
Proper 9 / Pent 7 / O T 14	Proper 14
Proper 10 / Pent 8 / O T 15	Proper 15
Proper 11 / Pent 9 / O T 16	Proper 16
Proper 12 / Pent 10 / O T 17	Proper 17
Proper 13 / Pent 11 / O T 18	Proper 18
Proper 14 / Pent 12 / O T 19	Proper 19
Proper 15 / Pent 13 / O T 20	Proper 20
Proper 16 / Pent 14 / O T 21	Proper 21
Proper 17 / Pent 15 / O T 22	Proper 22
Proper 18 / Pent 16 / O T 23	Proper 23
Proper 19 / Pent 17 / O T 24	Proper 24
Proper 20 / Pent 18 / O T 25	Proper 25
Proper 21 / Pent 19 / O T 26	Proper 26
Proper 22 / Pent 20 / O T 27	Proper 27
Proper 23 / Pent 21 / O T 28	Proper 28
Proper 24 / Pent 22 / O T 29	Proper 29
Proper 25 / Pent 23 / O T 30	Proper 30
Proper 26 / Pent 24 / O T 31	Proper 31
Proper 27 / Pent 25 / O T 32	Proper 32
Proper 28 / Pent 26 / O T 33	Proper 33
Christ The King (Proper 29 / O T 34)	Proper 34 / Christ The King / Reign Of Christ
Reformation Day (October 31)	Reformation Day (October 31)
All Saints' Day (November 1 or 1st Sunday in November)	All Saints' Day (November 1)
Thanksgiving Day (4th Thursday of November)	Thanksgiving Day (2nd Monday of October)

*O T = Ordinary Time

184

Contributors

Deborah (Deb) M. Alexander is the mother of two and grandmother of four. She is a member of Trinity United Methodist Church, Chesapeake City, Maryland, where she serves on the Staff/Parish Relations Committee and as co-leader of Mission Works. 105 Douglas St., Elkton, Maryland 21921. .

Kendall W. Anderson is a graduate of Bangor Theological Seminary and served pastorates in New England and Wisconsin before retiring in 1984. 501 First St. North, Skylight Gardens #202, St. Cloud, Minnesota 56303. kwandy@cloudnet.com.

Bonny Joy Bailey has been married to Thomas for ten years. They have four children, six grandchildren, four step-grandchildren, and three step-great-grandchildren. Bonny writes poetry and short stories. She is a member of Christ United Methodist Church in Greenfield, Wisconsin. She leads Companions In Christ classes and youth mission trips. Bonny retired in 1999 from GE Medical Systems after 25 years. 3435 W. Holmes Ave., Greenfield, Wisconsin 53221. bonnyjoy@tds.net.

William Bell was born and raised in Detroit, Michigan. He served two tours of duty in Vietnam from 1969-71. Bill graduated from the University of Michigan, and is employed in the field of facility management and development. He is a member of Wauwatosa Avenue United Methodist Church and resides with his family in the Milwaukee area. 4685 Lincrest Drive, Brookfield, Wisconsin 53045. bellifms@hotmail.com.

Christina Berry is a member of St. Andrew Presbyterian Church in Albuquerque, New Mexico, and a student at Austin Presbyterian Theological Seminary in Austin, Texas. For the past fifteen years, she has served Presbyterian churches as a volunteer, as children's ministry staff, and as a preacher and pastoral intern. Christina was the writer for the PC(USA) Children's Mission Yearbook for 2003 and for 2004, and a contributing writer to *Seasons of the Spirit* curriculum for 2005.

Cleveland B. Bishop, Sr. is pastor of First Christian Church (Disciples of Christ) in Raton, New Mexico. Cleve believes his calling is to promote effective, dynamic, evangelistic Christian life and to encourage Christians to be bold about their faith. 505-445-3931-Church, 505-445-8260-Parsonage. revcbbishop@hotmail.com, http://www.ratondisciples.com.

Judith B. Brain is the pastor of Pilgrim Congregational Church, United Church of Christ in Lexington, Massachusetts. A graduate of Harvard Divinity School, she loves mysteries, crossword puzzles, and gardening (she even has a sermon on compost!). Judy and her husband, Joe, enjoy kayaking. They have three sons and twin grandsons who keep them young and make them laugh.

Lois Ann Weihe Bross was born in Milwaukee, and grew up in Nachusa, Illinois, where her father, a Lutheran pastor, served as executive director of a children's home for 25 years. She has a degree in English from the University of Illinois, and she and her husband, Ed, have an adult son whom they adopted from Taiwan 21 years ago. Lois and Ed are members of St. Matthew's Lutheran Church in Wauwatosa, where they sing in the church choir and enjoy sharing major and minor pieces of liturgical stained glass that they create. 1505 Indianwood Dr., Brookfield, Wisconsin 53005, lwb14@juno.com.

Paul W. Calkin has served a variety of congregations in Oklahoma, Kansas, Nebraska, and Arkansas, and has served as Associate Pastor of First United Methodist Church, Edmond, Oklahoma, since June, 2003. pcalkineumc@sbcglobal.net.

Claire Clyburn is pastor of Calvary Memorial United Methodist Church in Snow Hill, North Carolina. She co-edited "Here I Am, Lord," a collection of essays by pastors describing the various ways

God called them into ministry, and has published sermons in an edition of the *Abingdon Preachers' Manual.* claireclyburn@earthlink.net.

Ned Dorau is a native of Milwaukee, Wisconsin, who earned his Masters of Divinity degree from St. Francis Seminary in Milwaukee after a first career in business. He served an internship in West Point, Nebraska, was assigned to the Wisconsin Synod, and accepted a parish in Random Lake, Wisconsin, where he is near family in suburban Milwaukee and close to longtime interests — like the Milwaukee Symphony and Florentine Opera, the Brewers, and Marquette basketball. NEDorau@aol.com.

Jim Eaton is the pastor of United Congregational Church in Norwich, Connecticut, a husband and father of three, grandfather of one. He has also served churches in Washington, Wisconsin, and Michigan. A graduate of Boston University School of Theology and Michigan State University, Jim came to ministry through theatre: "One day I realized a worship service was just a special kind of play." He loves sailing, good stories, and woodworking. Jim and his wife, Jacquelyn, work extensively with youth and oversee a Montessori preschool.

Vickie Eckoldt is a member of Wauwatosa Avenue United Methodist Church in Wauwatosa, Wisconsin. She and her husband, Al, have been married for 36 years and have one grown daughter, Pam, and a grandson, Travis. Vickie has had stories published in the first two editions of the *Vision Stories* series.

Marjorie K. Evans, a former elementary school teacher, is now a freelance writer with many published articles in Christian magazines, teacher's publications, and Sunday school papers. Her devotional articles have been included in sixteen devotional books. Marjorie attends Calvary Chapel of Lake Forest, California, enjoys her two sons, a daughter-in-law, and four grandchildren. She also enjoys reading and raising orchids. 4162 Fireside Circle, Irvine, California 92604.

Rev. Jody E. Felton is the pastor of First United Methodist Church in The Dalles, Oregon, just east of the Cascade Mountains on the banks of the beautiful Columbia River. The congregation of about seventy consists of teachers, farmers, and business people, many of whom are retired. She is a member of The Dalles Community Covenant Task Group that seeks to strengthen the community spiritually, emotionally, and physically. She has previously been published in *Alive Now* under the name Jody Wegener. 305 E. 11th Street, The Dalles, Oregon. 541-296-4675, fax 541-296-2134. jodyfelton@charter.net.

Barbara Frank has been a member of Grand Avenue United Methodist Church in Port Washington, Wisconsin, for twenty years. She works for a sales promotion agency, but lists her greatest accomplishments as being the mother of three sons and grandmother of two. Her story about healing was published in *Sharing Visions: Divine Revelations, Angels, And Holy Coincidences.*

Richard (Rick) H. Gentzler, Jr., is director of the Center on Aging and Older Adult Ministries for the General Board of Discipleship of The United Methodist Church. A much sought after speaker and seminar leader, Dr. Gentzler is nationally recognized as a teacher, writer, and leader in the field of aging and older adult ministries. He is the 2003 recipient of the National Interfaith Coalition on Aging (NICA) "Spirituality and Aging" Award, and is a member of the Society of Certified Senior Advisors. Dr. Gentzler is author of numerous books on adult and older adult ministry. His latest book, *The Graying Of The Church,* will be available in 2004. He publishes the *Center Sage* newsletter and has recently co-produced *Rock Of Ages,* a large-print worship and songbook. Dr. Gentzler is a clergy member of the Central Pennsylvania Conference of The United Methodist Church, and can be reached at the General Board of Discipleship — UMC, P.O. Box 340003, Nashville, Tennessee 37203-0003. 615-340-7173 or Toll Free: 877-788-2780 ext. 7173. Fax: 615-340-7071; rgentzler@gbod.org.

Elaine Klemm Grau is a retired psychotherapist, MSSW, UWM, spiritual director, MA, Sacred Heart School of Theology, Hales Corners, Wisconsin, Sacred Heart Congregation, Racine, Wisconsin, Eucharistic Minister, catechist, lector, communion presider, and President of Hickory Hollow Development. 4835 Richmond Drive, Racine, Wisconsin 53406. 262-637-2277. egrau@execpc.com.

Janice Hammerquist was born and raised in western South Dakota. She and her husband of forty years live on a ranch and have two children and seven grandchildren. Janice works as a legal secretary in the U.S. Attorney's Office and belongs to the South Maple United Methodist Church in Rapid City, South Dakota.

Theresa Hammerquist lives in New Berlin, Wisconsin, with her husband and three daughters. She holds degrees in Psychology and Spanish. Shortly after the events of "Kristina's Angel" occurred, Theresa began watercolor classes to fulfill a lifetime dream of illustrating and publishing children's books. Through these events and classes, Theresa discovered a latent artistic ability and created a note card business called Tricycle Creations. Her specialty is children's portraiture. She is a member of St. Elizabeth Ann Seton Catholic Church. tevahammerquist@aol.com.

Bonnie Compton Hanson, a former editor of Scripture Press, and curriculum writer and product designer with five other educational publishers, has served on the editorial staff of several Christian periodicals. Among the 23 books she has authored or co-authored is a finalist for a Gold Medallion Award, plus a popular new five-book *Ponytail Girls* Christian series for girls. Hundreds of her articles, poems, and other writings have been published in dozens of magazines and anthologies, including four *Chicken Soup For The Soul* books. Bonnie has also been a teacher, pastor's wife, missionary in Australia, and communications specialist for an international investment firm. She and her husband, Dr. Don J. Hanson, have three sons, four grandchildren, and a house and yard full of pets. Bonnie enjoys ministering through speaking, mentoring new writers, and serving in her local church. 3330 S. Lowell St., Santa Ana, California, 714-751-7824, bonnieh1@worldnet.att.net.

Linda Willis Harper was raised on a dairy farm in southwestern Wisconsin, and has had a story published in a book about cancer victims. After college, Linda taught elementary school for two years before her two children, Bruce and Brenda, were born. She then served as a substitute teacher for ten years. In 1975, Linda became a Mary Kay cosmetics consultant. She and her husband, Bob, retired to Arizona in 1998, where they attend the First Assembly of God Church. 1511 E. Florence Blvd., Casa Grande, Arizona 85222.

Martha Hartman is an ordained minister with the United Church of Christ and serves two churches, First Congregational Church, Russell, and Gorham Community Church, Gorham, in Kansas. She previously served as editor of several publications in Massachusetts and Pennsylvania, and taught English at Texas A&M University-Kingsville. Martha has had fiction and nonfiction published in more than thirty publications, including *These Days, Monday Morning, Vineyard Gazette,* and college journals.

Sandra Herrmann is pastor of Memorial United Methodist Church, Greenfield, Wisconsin. She has previously been published by CSS Publishing Company in a book of sermon starters titled *Ambassadors of Hope*, and has sermons included in *52 Sermon Stories*. 3450 S. 52nd St., Greenfield, Wisconsin 53219. 414-545-3969. RevSandra@wi.rr.com, Click the "Pastor" button on the website: www.MemorialUMC.org.

Lori Hetzel attends Christ United Methodist Church in Greenfield, Wisconsin. She has been married to her very best friend, Karl, for fifteen years, and is a stay-at-home mom, raising their two sons, Logan and Connor, and their three-and-a-half-year-old adopted daughter, Delaney. Lori has had stories in the previous two *Visions* books. lhetzel@wi.rr.com.

Gail C. Ingle passed June 13, 2004, at the age of 54. She had been on medical leave after teaching in the Waukesha, Wisconsin, school system since 1984. One of her stories appeared in *Sharing Visions: Divine Revelations, Angels, And Holy Coincidences.* Gail is a member of the Genesee United Congregational Church.

Susan D. Jamison is an ordained Elder in the Central Pennsylvania Conference of the United Methodist Church. In addition to serving in parish ministry, she has worked as a counselor with survivors of sexual abuse and domestic violence, and as a parent educator. She also works with the Sexual Misconduct Intervention Team for the church, and does prevention education workshops on clergy sexual misconduct. Susan has also done some mediation and healing ministry. sjamison@evenlink.com.

Kate Jones is an attorney and a United Methodist clergywoman serving in extension ministry as Chaplain and Director of Prevention Services at Women and Children's Horizons, Inc. in Kenosha, Wisconsin. Her ministry includes work with victims and perpetrators of domestic violence and survivors of sexual assault. Kate's previous publications include contributions to "Light Into Darkness," *Reflections for Advent and Epiphany, 2002,* November 2002, and "Growing Through Conflict," *Response* Magazine, co-authored with Thomas W. Porter, Jr. Kate lives in Kenosha with her husband, Robert, and their three children.

Tom Kadel is Senior Pastor of Christ Lutheran Church in Kulpsville, Pennsylvania. He is also a family therapist with a small private practice. Tom lives in Harleysville, Pennsylvania, with his wife, Lois, and his family, including grown children Bob, Liz, and Chris. Over his career, he has been a frequent contributor to church-related publications and has authored several catechetical courses for the Evangelical Lutheran Church in America. In the early '80s he edited the book, *Growth In Ministry,* which explored how clergy can be more effective in pastoring congregations.

191

Paul Karrer has had five of his stories in published in the *Chicken Soup for the Soul* series, and has sold the screen rights to one of his stories, *The Baby Flight*. He can be heard once a month reading on *First Person Singular,* Radio KUSP (88.9 FM) Santa Cruz, California. In January, 2004, two of his stories will be published in *Open My Eyes, Open My Soul,* by Yolanda King, daughter of Dr. Martin Luther King, Jr. Paul was a Peace Corps teacher in Western Samoa and taught in Korea, American Samoa, Connecticut, and England. He now lives in Monterey, California with his wife and ten-year-old daughter.

Harold Klug, of Cedar Grove, Wisconsin, is a retired farmer and a member of St. Paul's Lutheran Church in Random Lake.

Lisa Lancaster was ordained as a pastor in the Presbyterian Church (USA) in 1987. After pastoring a church for four years, she answered a call to specialized ministry as a chaplain, becoming Board Certified in the Association of Professional Chaplains in 1994. For the past eleven years she has served as Chaplain/Director of Pastoral Care at Central State Health Care System. She has taught on the topic "High Death Awareness" at a national conference. Lisa and her husband, Richard, a research meteorologist, live in Millstone Township, New Jersey, with their "four-legged children" (one cat, one dog), and enjoy traveling. LLancast@centrastate.com.

Cindy Loomis-Abell, an ordained minister in the United Methodist Church in Michigan, is the mother of three boys. She is also a liturgical artist, musician, and singer. Her work has been published in *Interpreter* magazine, *Inspirational Women* ezine, and *The Font,* the member publication for the Order of St. Luke, of which she has been a member since 1997. revcala@hotmail.com.

J. Michael Mansfield, a native of Florida, is an Elder in the Kentucky Conference of the United Methodist Church. He is a graduate of the University of Kentucky and United Theological Seminary of Dayton, Ohio. Mike serves the Dixon/Dixie Charge in the Madisonville District. He co-authored "The First Female United

Methodist Elder (Ella Niswonger)," published in *The Religious Telescope,* with Donald K. Gorrell. Mike and his wife, Gay, have one son, Jim, and one granddaughter, Paige.

LaNette J. McQuitty, CD, CLA, CBE, is a birth doula in private practice. As a Professional Labor Assistant and HypnoBirthing Practitioner she has had the honor of attending at over 200 births. She believes that birth is a deeply spiritual and joyful experience that impacts a woman's entire life. As a doula, she provides the loving atmosphere that will make the journey to motherhood as empowering and fulfilling as God intended it to be. LaNette is the creator of the world's first patented board game about pregnancy, *Who's Having This Baby Anyway?,* and the owner of the website www.babygame.com. She also produced the birth video, "The Power of Birth." LaNette is a member of the Association of Labor Assistants and Childbirth Educators (ALACE), Doulas of North America (DONA), and the Childbirth Assistance Resources and Education (C.A.R.E.) Network.

Ralph Milton has worked in Christian communication most of his adult life, serving in the Philippines, New York, and in his native Canada. He is a co-founder of Canada's largest religious publishing house, Wood Lake Books, and is himself the author of more than a dozen books. Milton edits a weekly on-line magazine of humor and faith called *Rumors,* which is available free by sending an e-mail note to him at ralphmilton@woodlake.com. His efforts in Christian communication, especially his work in the field of humor and faith, have brought him two honorary doctorates from Canadian theological schools.

Susan Monnarjahn has been involved in the spiritually-based recovery community for the past ten years, working with others to overcome various addictions. She lives in New Orleans, Louisiana, with her husband and two cats. SRose12286@aol.com.

Jane Moschenrose, a graduate of Andover Newton Theological School, has served as pastor of Wellspring Church, an American

Baptist Church in Farmington, Michigan, since 1998. She is married to Phillip and mother of Karen. 1133 Elliott Court, Madison Heights, Michigan 48071. jmoschenro@aol.com.

Nancy Nichols, a United Methodist minister, has written teenage pregnancy prevention curriculum, worked in a welfare-to-work program, and taught parenting skills to at risk parents. In addition to serving St. Paul's United Methodist Church in Muncie, Indiana, Nancy has finished course work toward a Doctorate of Education and is starting her dissertation on United Methodist women clergy ordained in North Indiana from 1974-1990. She also teaches several courses at the local community college. She still finds time for good friends, good coffee, good food, good rock and roll dance bands, and three dogs. Nancy's call story was published in *Vision Stories: True Accounts Of Visions, Angels, And Healing Miracles*.

Andrew Oren lives in Milwaukee, Wisconsin, with his wife, Julie. They have three grown children. Andy is pastor of Faith United Methodist Church, also in Milwaukee, a role that has been the result of a long process of discerning God's call in his life. He spent 26 years in manufacturing before leaving in 1999 to become a Lay Minister in the United Methodist Church. 3156 S. Kin-nickinnic Ave., Milwaukee, Wisconsin 53207. aoren@wi.rr.com.

Carolyn Peake is working as part-time interim pastor for the chapel of a retirement home in Williamstown, Vermont. She attends Northfield United Methodist Church in Northfield, Vermont, is a certified lay speaker, and is training to become a spiritual director. carpeake@nfld.tds.net.

Ruth F. Piotter, 88, is a resident of the Lutheran Home in Fond du Lac, Wisconsin. Her family includes four daughters, ten grandchildren, and seven great-grandchildren. She enjoys reading, doing crossword puzzles, and corresponding via e-mail with friends and family all over the country. Ruth just completed her forty-eighth year of keeping a daily diary. She is a member of Immanuel-Trinity Lutheran Church, where her late husband, Paul, served as senior pastor from 1956-1990.

Kathy Raines is pastor of Jefferson United Methodist Church in Jefferson, Oregon. She is an ordained elder in the United Methodist Church and has served as senior pastor, co-pastor, and associate pastor in rural and town churches in Oregon and Iowa. Kathy earned a Masters of Divinity degree from United Theological Seminary in Dayton, Ohio, in 1988. She is married to the Reverend John David Raines, and they are the parents of two children. 1020 Hermanson St., Woodburn, Oregon 97071. 503-981-2992. RainesJD@cs.com.

William Lee Rand, founder of the International Center for Reiki Training, and author of *Reiki, The Healing Touch, Reiki For A New Millennium,* and *The Spirit Of Reiki* (along with Arjava Petter and Walter Lubeck), is a Reiki Master of the Usui lineage and developer of Karuna Reiki. He has 25 years of experience in metaphysics and healing work, and was initiated into Reiki on the big island of Hawaii in 1981. He is the editor of the *Reiki News* magazine and teaches Reiki classes worldwide. www.reiki.org, The International Center for Reiki Training, 21421 Hilltop #28, Southfield, Michigan 48034. 800-332-8112. center@reiki.org. A new website for Christians who practice Reiki can be found at www.christianreiki.org.

R. Ellen Rasmussen is the Director of Christian Nurture and Family Ministries at Covenant United Methodist Church in Fond du Lac, Wisconsin, and an Independent Grand Achiever Car Driver with Mary Kay Cosmetics, Inc. Ellen and her two children, Erika and Joey, reside at 20 N. Marr St., Fond du Lac, Wisconsin. 920-921-4949; fax 920-921-2253, ellenrasmussen@wisconsinumc.org.

Marie Regine Redig, SSND is semi-retired. She left Mount Mary College and the Ewens Center, Milwaukee, Wisconsin, and now ministers part time as a retreat/spiritual director. She serves on the Leadership Team for Associates connected to the School Sisters of Notre Dame in the Milwaukee Province, and is a member of Mary, Queen of Martyrs Roman Catholic Church. 4244 N. 50th St., Milwaukee, Wisconsin 53216. rredig@ssnd-milw.org.

Derrick Sanderson is a junior at Viterbo University in LaCrosse, Wisconsin, majoring in biology with a minor in Environmental Studies. He is a member of St. Aiden's Episcopal Church in Hartford, Wisconsin, and a proud counselor of the United Methodist summer camp YO-MI-CA (Youth Mission Camp). dsanderson@email.com.

Joyce Schroer is the pastor of First Congregational Church and Society UCC, in Berlin Heights, Ohio. She is certified as a specialist in Christian Education through the United Church of Christ. Joyce is active on the Church Development Team of the Northwest Ohio Association, and serves on the Board of Directors of the United Church Homes.

Maria Seifert is a writer by trade. She was recently pushed by God to share some of her miracles, write about the importance of prayer, and provide humorous soul-seeking messages through her writing. She has written a children's book titled *Ava's Angels* and is working on an *Ava's Angels* series. Maria is from Milwaukee and attends Elmbrook Church. She has been happily married for eight and a half years and has three children. Maria_Seifert@yahoo.com.

Kathleen A. Slawski has been known as "Kit" forever. She and her husband, Robb, have three sons, Andrew, fifteen, Ryan, eleven, and Daniel, six, and are members of Christ the King Catholic Church in Wauwatosa, Wisconsin. Kit returned to work as Sales Office Manager at Raabe Corporation in Menomonee Falls, Wisconsin, after being a stay-at-home mom for ten years. She has always been an active volunteer in many parish and school activities.

David Michael Smith is the Christian author of one suspenseful novel and a joyous collection of touching Christmas short stories. He has also had several stories published in a variety of books including the *Cup Of Comfort* series. Mr. Smith attends church at Trinity Cathedral in Berlin, Maryland, with his wife, Geralynn. The Smiths also plan to adopt a daughter, Rebekah Joy, from China, in 2004. For more about David and his writing, visit his web page: http://www.davidmichaelsmith.net. He can be contacted at: 3 Oak Knoll Court, Georgetown, Delaware, 19947. davidandgeri@hotmail.com.

April McClure Stewart is an ordained minister in the Christian Church (Disciples of Christ) and is the pastor of First Christian Church of Rock Falls, Illinois. She attended Eureka College, Eureka, Illinois, and Lexington Theological Seminary, Lexington, Kentucky. She and her husband, Dennis, reside in Rock Falls. fccrockfalls@essex1.com.

Kay Boone Stewart is a novelist (*Trilogy, Chariots Of Dawn,* E. Thomas Nelson, '92), poet (*Sunrise Over Galilee,* '93), non-fiction writer (*Here's Help,* '93), collaborator (*Don Stewart Tips ...* '93, *Window Watchman 11,* CIN '97), artist (Kay Cards — 2001), music composer, harpist, vocalist, storyteller, member/deacon Presbyterian Church, *Who's Who America* (2002). P. O. Box 727, Brentwood, California 94513.

Karen Steineke was a resident of Wauwatosa, Wisconsin, from 1960 until 1989, where she, her husband, Ed, and their four children attended Wauwatosa Avenue United Methodist Church. Karen and Ed divide their retirement time between Wautoma, Wisconsin, and Surprise, Arizona, and attend United Methodist churches in both places.

John Sumwalt is pastor of Wauwatosa Avenue United Methodist Church. He is the author of the acclaimed series, *Lectionary Stories,* '90, '91, '92, published by CSS Publishing Company. John has co-authored two books with his wife, Jo, *Life Stories,* '95 and *Lectionary Tales For The Pulpit,* '96. He does storytelling, inspirational speaking, and retreats. 2044 Forest Street, Wauwatosa, Wisconsin 53213. 414-257-1228. Fax: 414-453-0702. jsumwalt@naspa.net.

Anne Sunday is a native of Harrisburg, Pennsylvania, and a graduate of Lancaster Theological Seminary, Lancaster, Pennsylvania. She is pastor of First United Church of Christ of Pleasant Valley in rural Clarksville, Iowa. Anne's passion in ministry is leading Confirmation and adult Bible study classes. She writes devotional articles for a local community newspaper. While serving a church in Huntington, West Virginia, she participated in a Life Writing Tutorial at the Huntington Museum of Art and had a story published in The Life Writing Class, edited by John Patrick Grace of Publishers Place. She lives with her German Shepherd dog, in the church parsonage, located on a gravel road across from the church at 14967 Vail Avenue, Clarksville, Iowa 50619. 319-276-3066. RevSunday@butler-bremer.com.

Pamela J. Tinnin is the pastor of Partridge Community Church — UCC, the only church in Partridge, Kansas (population 250). She was an editor at the University of California-Berkley, for ten years, a freelance writer, and a sheep rancher. Recently, Pam collaborated with two United Methodist pastors on a collection of dramatic monologue sermons, *Bit Players In The Big Play*, CSS Publishing Company, 2004. Pam also had a story included in *Sharing Visions: Divine Revelations, Angels, And Holy Coincidences* in 2003.

Rosmarie Trapp is a member of the "Community of the Crucified One," 104 E. 11th Avenue, Homestead, Pennsylvania 15120. She lives in an apartment in one of their mission houses in Vermont, where she is involved in children's Bible classes, fund raisers, and prison ministry, sharing the message, "Jesus loves you." Her family's story was told in the well-known movie, *The Sound Of Music*. Rosmarie has also had stories included in the first two editions of *Vision Stories*.

Larry Winebrenner is Professor Emeritus of Miami-Dade Community College, after 33 years of teaching. He served as pastor of churches in Georgia, Florida, Indiana, and Wisconsin, retiring after thirteen years as pastor of York Memorial UMC in Miami. He serves as Chaplain of Epworth Village Retirement Community in Hialeah, Florida. Larry has authored two college textbooks, served as an editor for three newspapers and an academic journal, and contributed articles to several magazines.

Laurie Woodard calls herself a Disciple of Christ skillfully disguised as a wife, mother of five, and substitute teacher. She recently completed a Three-Year Program of Spiritual Formation sponsored by the United Methodist Church. Her favorite pastimes are hiking, biking, and reading spiritual classics. She is a member of the First United Methodist Church of Waukesha, Wisconsin. angel3762@aol.com.

Praise for *Sharing Visions* and *Vision Stories*,
John Sumwalt's previous collections of
true personal accounts of mystical experiences:

I am rejoicing as I read these testimonies. What an inspiration! I recall my father, an unemotional man, telling me that his mother who had died some years before appeared to him in a dream and gave him counsel on a difficult decision he was wrestling with.
 Bishop Richard B. Wilke
 Co-creator of the *Disciple* Bible Study series

At long last someone has demonstrated the courage to lift the veil of silence that so often covers the mystical experiences of ordinary people. By denying the reality of these experiences we have denied spiritual sustenance and growth to many. **Vision Stories** *is a forerunner of the feast that is to come for all who earnestly seek to walk with God.*
 Bishop Reuben P. Job
 Author of *A Guide to Spiritual Discernment*
 Former editor, *The Upper Room*

This dynamic, moving, and deeply authentic collection of true stories will carry readers on a powerful journey of healing and inspiration. **Sharing Visions** *will appeal to Catholic and Protestant alike.*
 Deacon Eddie Ensley
 Author of *Visions: The Soul's Path To The Sacred*

Through stories and scriptural comparisons, Sumwalt offers insight into the extraordinary spiritual experiences of ordinary people.
 Cheryl Kirking
 Author of *Ripples of Joy*

John Sumwalt has given us a treasury of God's meetings with the daily lives of people. Too often we think of God as hidden away in the stories of the Bible. Here we see God now encountering people in surprising ways of grace. May these stories encourage us to tell one another our stories of God's meetings with us as well.

    Dwight Judy
    Author of *Quest for the Mystical Christ*

*I am very impressed with **Vision Stories** as a resource for preaching, teaching, and spiritual formation reading. People, myself included, are hesitant to share holy moments which we think may seem strange to others. We fear they may not be received with the sanctity and gratitude which will always surround these moments for us. But others need to hear such stories, shared for no other reason than to witness to the reality of God in personal experience. This is what **Vision Stories** invites all of us to do. These stories help us to meet what may be the greatest spiritual need of our time — to know and to share the experience of the reality of God and the spiritual realm in a materialistic world.*

    Charles R. Gipson
    Author of *The Three-Year Community for Spiritual Formation*

Reading through these accounts forces the realization that the world in which we live is far more mysterious than we realize, and the realm of God's grace far deeper and richer than we can imagine. These experiences will be a great encouragement to many, especially those who have had such experiences but have thought they were abnormal.

    M. Robert Mulholland
    Author of *Shaped by the Word*